The First Seven Divisions

The First Seven Divisions

A Detailed Account of the Fighting
from Mons to Ypres During the
Great War, 1914-1918

Ernest W. Hamilton

LEONAUR

The First Seven Divisions: a Detailed Account of the Fighting from Mons to Ypres During the Great War, 1914-1918
by Ernest W. Hamilton

Leonaur is an imprint of Oakpast Ltd

Material original to this edition and presentation of the text in this form copyright © 2012 Oakpast Ltd

ISBN: 978-0-85706-912-2 (hardcover)
ISBN: 978-0-85706-913-9 (softcover)

http://www.leonaur.com

Publisher's Notes

Contents

THE FOLLOWING ABBREVIATIONS HAVE BEEN
USED IN THIS BOOK:

The C. in C. = Field Marshal Sir John French
A.C. = Army Corps
C.B. = Cavalry Brigade
K.O.S.B. = King's Own Scottish Borderers
K.O.Y.L.I. = King's Own Yorkshire Light Infantry
K.R.R. = King's Royal Rifles (60th)

Preface

The 1st Expeditionary Force to leave England consisted of the 1st A.C. (1st and 2nd Divisions) and the 2nd A.C. (3rd and 5th Divisions). The 4th Division arrived in time to prolong the battle-front at Le Cateau, but it missed the terrible stress of the first few days, and can therefore hardly claim to rank as part of the 1st Expeditionary Force in the strict sense. The 6th Division did not join till the battle of the Aisne. These two divisions then formed the 3rd A.C.

In the following pages the doings of the 3rd A.C. are only very lightly touched upon, not because they are less worthy of record than those of the 1st and 2nd A.C., but simply because they do not happen to have come within the field of vision of the narrator.

The 7th Division's doings are dealt with because these were inextricably mixed up with the operations of the 1st A.C. east of Ypres. The 3rd A.C., on the other hand, acted throughout as an independent unit, and had no part in the Ypres and La Bassée fighting with which these pages are attempting to deal.

The main point aimed at is accuracy; no attempt is made to magnify achievements, or to minimise failures.

It must, however, be clearly understood that the mention from time to time of certain battalions as having been driven from their trenches does not in the smallest degree suggest inefficiency on the part of such battalions. It is probable that every battalion in the British Force has at some time or another during the past twelve months been forced to abandon its trenches. A battalion is driven from its trenches as often as not owing to insupportable shell-fire concentrated on a particular area. Such trenches may be afterwards retaken by another battalion under entirely different circumstances, and in any case in the absence of shell-fire. That goes without saying. It may, therefore, quite easily happen that lost trenches may be retaken by a battalion which is inferior in all military essentials to the battalion which was driven out of the same trenches the day before, or earlier in the same day, as the case may be.

I wish to take this opportunity of expressing the great obligations under which I lie to the many officers who have so kindly assisted me in the compilation of this work.

CHAPTER 1

Before Mons

When an entire continent has for eighteen months been convulsed by military operations on so vast a scale as almost to baffle imagination, the individual achievements of this division or of that division are apt to fade quickly out of recognition. Fresh scenes peopled by fresh actors hold the public eye, and, in the quick passage of events, the lustre of bygone deeds soon gets blurred. People forget. But when the deeds are such as to bring a thrill of national pride; when they set up an all but unique standard of valour for future generations to live up to, it is best not to forget.

On the outbreak of war with Germany on August 3rd, 1914, the British army was so small as to be a mere drop in the ocean of armed men who were hurrying to confront one another on the plains of Belgium. It was derisively described as "contemptible." And yet, in the first three months of the war, this little army, varying in numbers from 80,000 to 130,000, may justly claim to have in some part moulded the history of Europe. It was the deciding factor in a struggle where the sides—at first—were none too equally matched. For this alone its deeds are worthy of record, and they are worthy of record too for another reason. They represent the supreme sacrifice in the interests of the national honour of what was familiarly known as our "regular army." Since the outbreak of the war, fresh armies have arisen, of new and unprecedented proportions. The members of these new armies are as familiar now to the public eye as the representatives of the old regular army are scarce. With the doings of these new armies the present pages have no concern. They are, it is true, the expression of a spirit of patriotism and duty so remarkable that their voluntary growth must for ever stand out as one of the grandest monuments in the history of Britain. But they form no part of the subject matter of these pages, which deal solely with the way in which the old regular army, led by the best in the land, saved the national honour in the acutest crisis in history, and practically ceased to exist in the doing of it.

The regular army, small as it was, did not lie under the hands of those who would use it. Much of it was far away across the seas, guarding the outposts of the Empire. A certain proportion, however, was at hand, and with a smoothness and expedition which silenced, no less than it amazed, the critics of our military administration, 50,000 infantry, with its artillery and five brigades of cavalry, were shipped off to France almost before the public had realized that we were at war. From Havre or Boulogne, as the case might be, these troops either marched or were trained northwards; shook themselves into shape; gradually assumed the form of two army corps of two divisions each, of which the 1st Division was on the right and the 5th on the left (the 4th Division having not yet arrived), and in this formation faced the Belgian frontier to meet and check the invaders.

The two advancing forces met at Mons, or, to be more accurate, the British force took up a defensive position at Mons—in conformity with the pre-arranged plan of extending the French line westwards—and there waited.

From this time on, the doings of the Expeditionary Force become historically interesting, and its movements are worthy of study in detail. In the first instance, however, in order to arrive at a proper understanding of the circumstances which governed the position of the British troops on the occasion of their first stand, and which afterwards dictated the line of retreat and the roads to be followed in that retreat, and the successive points at which the retreating army faced about and fought, it is desirable to get a general grasp of the geographical side of things. The Germans were advancing from the north-east on Paris; that was their avowed intention; there was no secret about it; the leaders openly proclaimed their intentions; the soldiers advertised the fact in chalk legends scribbled on the doors of the houses; and—as the fashion is with Germans in arms—they were taking the most direct route to their objective, their artillery and transport following the great main roads that shoot out north-eastward from Paris towards Brussels, with their infantry swarming in endless thousands along the smaller collateral roads. Here and there, at intervals of from twenty to thirty miles, this system of parallel roads running north-east from Paris is crossed by other main roads running at right angles and forming, as it were, a skeleton check with the point of the diamond to the north. These main cross-roads had, in anticipation, been selected for the lines of defence along which our troops should turn and fight if necessary, for though it is laid down in the text-books of the wise that a line of defence must not run along a main road, such a road has obvious value for purposes of correct alignment. As the German advance was from the north-east, it is self-evident that the line of resistance or defence had to extend from north-west to south-east.

When our troops, by forced marches, reached Mons on August 22nd, 1914, the primary business of the British Force was to prolong the French line of resistance in a north-westerly direction. The natural country feature which was geographically indicated for this purpose was the high road which runs from Charleroi through Binche to Mons, and this was the line for which our troops were originally destined. In effect, however, this line proved to be impracticable, for the simple reason that, when we reached it, the Germans were already in possession of Charleroi, and the French on our right had fallen back beyond the point of prolongation of this line. For the British force in these circumstances to have occupied the Mons—Charleroi road would have laid it open to the very great risk—if not certainty—of being cut off and completely isolated. In these circumstances there was no alternative but to range our 1st A.C. along the Mons—Beaumont road, in rear of the original position contemplated, while the 2nd A.C. lined the canal between Mons and Condé. The position was not ideal, the formation being that of a broad arrow, with the two army corps practically at right angles to one another. However, it was the best that offered in the peculiar circumstances of the case. As it turned out in the end, the entire attack at Mons fell on the 2nd A.C., which lay back at an angle of forty-five degrees from the general line of defence. The battle of Mons may, therefore, in a sense be looked upon as an attempt at a flanking or enveloping movement on the part of the enemy, which was frustrated by the interposition of our troops.

In view of the fact that the scene of the first shock with the enemy was fixed by necessity and not by choice, the Mons canal may be considered as a fortunate feature in the landscape. It ran sufficiently true to the required line to offer an obvious line of defence, and an ideal one, except for the flagrant defect that, after running from Condé to Mons in a mathematically straight line, on reaching the town it flings off to the north in a loop some two miles long by one and a half miles across. This loop, as well as the straight reach to Condé, was occupied by our troops. The formation of the British army, then, was not only that of a broad arrow, but of a broad arrow with a loop two miles long by a mile and a half across projecting from the point. Such a position could obviously not be held for long, and Sir Horace Smith-Dorrien, recognizing this, had prepared in advance a second and more defensible line running through Frameries, Paturages, Wasmes and Boussu. To this second line the troops were to fall back as soon as the salient became untenable. A glance at the map will serve to show that the effect of swinging back the right of the 2nd A.C. to this new position would be to at once bring the whole British army into line, with a frontage facing the advance of the enemy from the north-east. In view, however, of the preparedness of the Germans and the comparative unpreparedness of the Allies, time was a factor in the case of the very first importance, and therefore the passage of the canal had to be opposed, if only for purposes of delay. It is important, however, to keep in mind that the real line which it was intended to defend at Mons was this second line. The intention was never carried out, because it was anticipated by an unexpected and most unwelcome order to retire in conformity with French movements on the right, which upset all plans.

In the meanwhile, the enemy's entry into Mons itself had to be delayed as long as possible, which meant that the canal salient, bad as it was, had perforce to be defended. This dangerous but most responsible duty was entrusted to Sir Hubert Hamilton with his 3rd Division, and, as a matter of fact, the battle of Mons in the end proved to be practically confined to the three brigades of this division.

The disposition of the division was as follows:

General Shaw, with the 9th Brigade, was posted along the western face of the canal loop, his right-hand battalion being the 4th R. Fusiliers, who held the line from the Nimy bridge, at Lock 6, to the Ghlin bridge. To the left of the R. Fusiliers, were the R. Scots Fusiliers, and beyond them again half the Northumberland Fusiliers reaching as far as Jemappes. The Lincolns and the rest of the Northumberland Fusiliers formed the reserve to the brigade and were at Cuesmes in rear of the canal.

On the right of the 9th Brigade was the 8th Brigade, occupying the north-east face of the canal salient. Of this brigade the 4th Middlesex on the left took up the line from the R. Fusiliers east of the Nimy bridge, and carried it on as far as the bridge and railway station at Obourg. Between Obourg and St. Symphorien were the 1st Gordon Highlanders, and on their right, thrown back so as to link up with the left of the 1st A.C., were the 2nd Royal Scots. The Royal Irish Regiment formed the brigade reserve at Hyon, and the 7th Brigade the divisional reserve at Cipley. So much then for the salient itself on which, as it turned out, the enemy's attack was mainly focussed. On the left of the 3rd Division, along the straight reach of the canal which runs to Condé, was Sir Charles Fergusson's 5th Division. Of this division we need only concern ourselves with the 13th Brigade, which continued the line of defence on the left of the 9th Brigade, the R. West Kents holding the ground from Mariette to Lock 5 at St. Ghislain, with the K.O.S.B. extended beyond them as far as Lock 4 at Les Herbières. The K.O.Y.L.I. and Duke of Wellington's Regiment were in reserve. On the left of the K.O.S.B. was the E. Surrey Regiment and beyond again the 14th and 15th Brigades. Later on the line was still further extended to the west by the 19th Brigade, which arrived during the afternoon of the 23rd.

Such then was the disposition of the 2nd A.C. The 1st A.C. lay back, as has been explained, almost at right angles to the line of the canal, along the two roads that branch off from Mons to Beaumont and Maubeuge respectively. On the first-named road was the 1st

Division reaching as far as Grand Reng. This division, however, as events turned out, was merely a spectator of the operations of August 23rd. The 2nd Division was very much scattered, the 6th Brigade being at Givry, and the 5th at Bougnies, while of the 4th Brigade the two Coldstream Battalions were at Harveng and the rest of the brigade at Quévy.

The gap between the 1st and 2nd A.C. was patrolled by the 2nd C.B., an operation which brought about the first actual collision between British and German troops. This was on the 22nd near Villers St. Ghislain, when Captain Hornby with a squadron of the 4th Dragoon Guards fell in with a column of Uhlans, which he promptly charged and very completely routed, capturing a number of prisoners.

The rest of our cavalry was spread along the Binche road as a covering screen for the 1st A.C., with the exception of the 4th C.B. which was at Haulchin cross-roads, guarding the approach to that place from the direction of Binche, and at the same time keeping up a communication between the 1st and 2nd Divisions.

Such then was, generally speaking, the position on August 22nd. During that night, however, all the cavalry was withdrawn from the Binche road and moved across to the left of our line, where they took up a position guarding that flank along the two roads running north and south through Thulin and Eloges to Andregnies. The 4th C.B., having the shortest journey to make, went four miles further west again to Quiverain. This change of position meant a twenty mile night march for the cavalry on the top of a hard day's patrol work, and the journey took them from six o'clock in the evening till two o'clock the following morning.

CHAPTER 2

The Battle of Mons

The morning of the 23rd opened sunny and bright. The weather was set fair with a breeze from the east, a cloudless sky, and the promise of great heat at midday. A pale blue haze rounded off the distance, and softened the outlines of the tall, gaunt chimney stacks with which the entire country is dotted.

With the first streak of dawn came the first German shell. It was evident from the outset that the canal loop had been singled out as the object of the enemy's special attentions. Its weakness from the defensive point of view was clearly as well known to them as it was to our own generals. It was also fairly obvious to both sides that, if the enemy succeeded in crossing the canal in the neighbourhood of the salient, the line of defence along the straight reach to Condé would have to be abandoned. The straight reach of the canal was therefore, for the time being, neglected, and all efforts confined to the salient. The bombardment increased in volume as the morning advanced and as fresh German batteries arrived on the scene, and at 8 a.m. came the first infantry attack.

This first attack was launched against the north-west corner of the canal loop, the focus-point being—as had been anticipated—the Nimy bridge, on which the two main roads from Lens and Soignies converge. The attack, however, soon became more general and the pressure quickly extended for a good mile and a half to either side of the Nimy bridge, embracing the railway bridge and the Ghlin bridge to the left of it, and the long reach to the Obourg bridge on the right.

The northern side of the canal is here dotted, throughout the

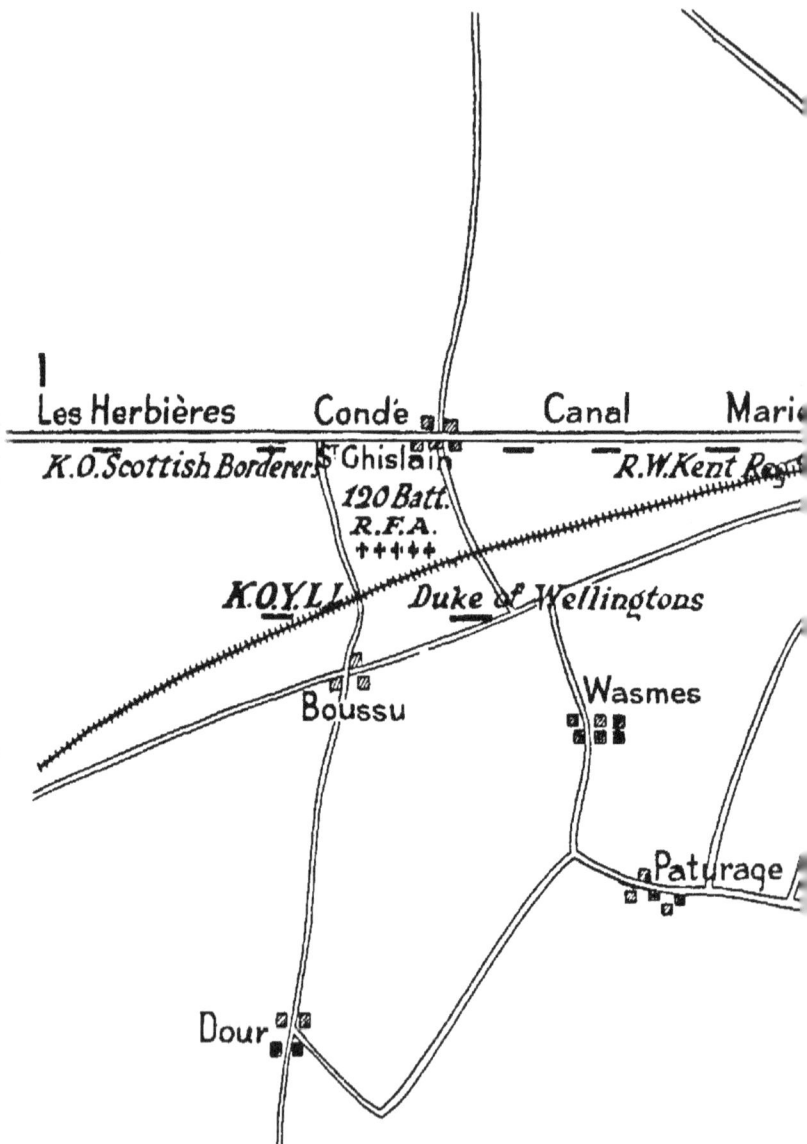

Les Herbières   Condé   Canal   Mari

K.O.Scottish Borderers. S¹ Ghislain   *R.W.Kent Reg*

120 Batt.
R.F.A.
+ + + + +

K.O.Y.L.I   *Duke of Wellingtons*

Wasmes

Boussu

Paturage

Dour

MAP SHOWING DISPOSITION OF TROOPS AT THE BATTLE OF MONS

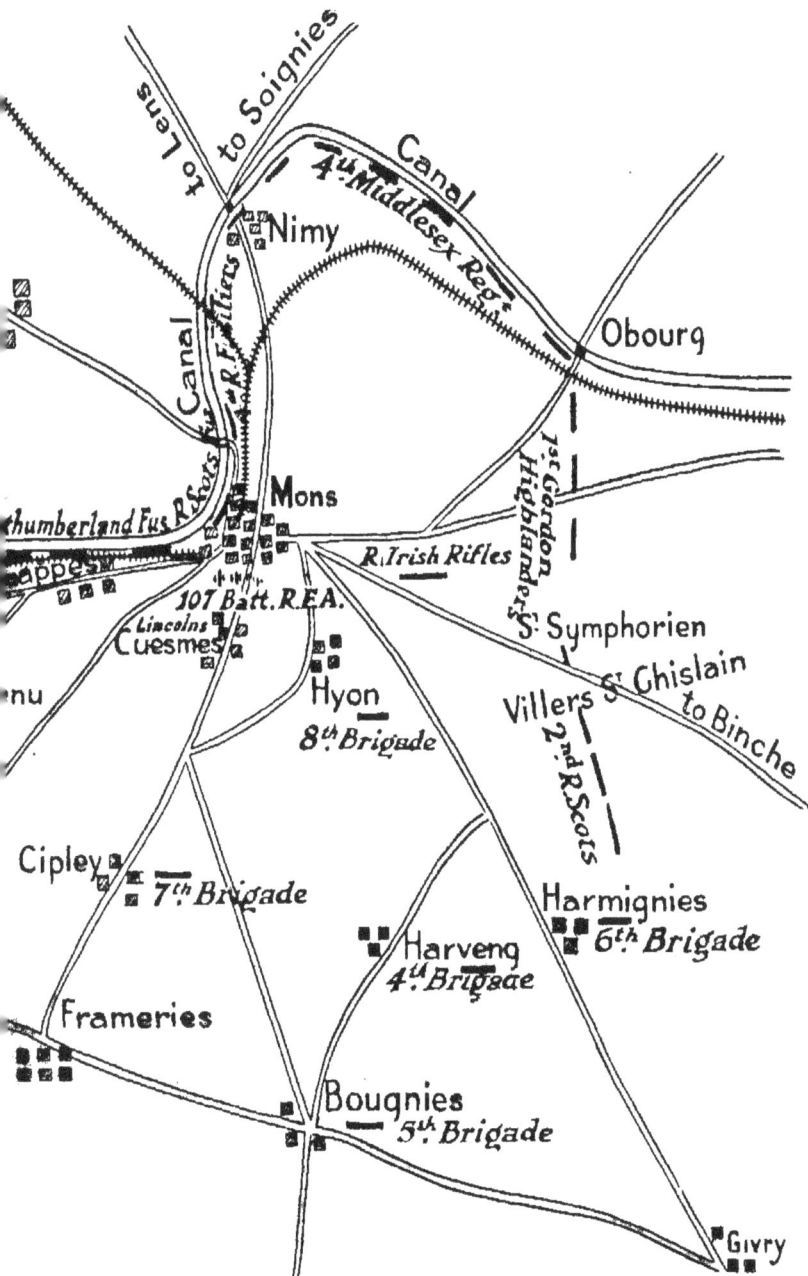

to Soignies

to Lens

Canal

4th Middlesex Regt.

Nimy

Canal

R. Scots Fus.

4th R. Fusiliers

Obourg

1st Gordon Highlanders

Sappers

humberland Fus.

Mons

R. Irish Rifles

St. Symphorien

107 Batt. R.F.A.

Lincolns

Cuesmes

St. Ghislain

Villers

to Binche

nu

Hyon

8th Brigade

2nd R. Scots

Cipley

7th Brigade

Harmignies

6th Brigade

Harveng

4th Brigade

Frameries

Bougnies

5th Brigade

Givry

entire length of the attacked position, with a number of small fir plantations which proved of inestimable value to the enemy for the purpose of masking their machine-gun fire, as well as for massing their infantry preparatory to an attack.

About nine o'clock the German infantry attack, which had been threatening for some time past, took definite shape and four battalions were suddenly launched upon the head of the Nimy bridge. The bridge was defended by a single company of the R. Fusiliers under Captain Ashburner and a machine-gun in charge of Lieutenant Dease.

The Germans attacked in close column, an experiment which, in this case proved a conspicuous failure, the leading sections going down as one man before the concentrated machine-gun and rifle fire from the bridge. The survivors retreated with some haste behind the shelter of one of the plantations, where they remained for half an hour. Then the attack was renewed, this time in extended order. The alteration in the formation at once made itself felt on the defenders. This time the attack was checked but not stopped. Captain Ashburner's company on the Nimy bridge began to be hard pressed and 2nd Lieutenant Mead was sent up with a platoon to its support. Mead was at once wounded—badly wounded in the head. He had it dressed in rear and returned to the firing line, to be again almost immediately shot through the head and killed. Captain Bowdon-Smith and Lieutenant Smith then went up to the bridge with another platoon.

Within ten minutes both had fallen badly wounded. Lieutenant Dease who was working the machine-gun had already been hit three times. Captain Ashburner was wounded in the head, and Captain Forster, in the trench to the right of him, had been shot through the right arm and stomach. The position on the Nimy bridge was growing very desperate, and it was equally bad further to the left, where Captain Byng's company on the Ghlin bridge was going through a very similar experience. Here again the pressure was tremendous and the Germans made considerable headway, but could not gain the bridges, Private Godley with his machine-gun sticking to his post to the very end, and doing tremendous execution. The defenders too had most effective support from the 107th Battery R.F.A. entrenched behind them, the

Artillery Observer in the firing line communicating the enemy's range with great accuracy.

To the right of the Nimy bridge the 4th Middlesex were in the meanwhile putting up a no less stubborn defence, and against equally desperate odds. Major Davey, whose company was on the left, in touch with the right of the R. Fusiliers, had fallen wounded early in the day, and the position at that point finally became so serious that Major Abell's company was rushed up from reserve to its support. During this advance Major Abell himself, Captain Knowles and 2nd Lieutenant Henstock were killed, and a third of the rank and file fell, but the balance succeeded in reaching the firing line trenches and—with this stiffening added—the position was successfully held for the time being.

Captain Oliver's company, in the centre of the Middlesex line, was also very hard pressed, and Colonel Cox sent up two companies of the R. Irish Regiment (who were in reserve at Hyon) to its support, another half company of the same regiment being at the same time sent to strengthen the right of the Middlesex line at the Obourg bridge, where Captain Roy had already been killed and Captain Glass wounded. The Gordons, on the right of the Middlesex, also suffered severely, but the Royal Scots beyond them were just outside of the zone of pressure, and their casualties were few.

The attack along the straight reach of the canal towards Condé was less violent, and was not pressed till much later in the day. Here, lining the canal towards the west, was the 5th Division (13th, 14th and 15th Brigades). On the right of this division and in touch with the Northumberland Fusiliers, who were the left-hand battalion of the 9th Brigade (in the 3rd Division) were the 1st R. West Kents. This battalion had on the previous day, in its capacity as advance guard to the brigade, been thrown forward as a screen some distance to the north of the canal, where it sustained some fifty casualties, Lieutenants Anderson and Lister being killed and 2nd Lieutenant Chitty wounded. Eventually, as the enemy advanced, the battalion was withdrawn to the south side of the canal, and on the 23rd it occupied the reach from Mariette on the east to the Pommeroeul—St. Ghislain road on the west, where two companies held the bridge at the lock. This position, however, was not seriously pressed, and the battalion had few further casualties during the day, though Captain Buchanon-Dunlop had the misfortune to be wounded by a shell at the outset of the attack.

Towards midday the attack against the straight reach of the canal became general. The whole line was shelled, and the German infantry, taking advantage of the cover afforded by the numerous fir plantations—which here, as at Nimy, dotted the north side of the canal—worked up to within a few hundred yards of the water, and from the cover of the trees maintained a constant rifle and machine-gun fire on the defenders.

About 3 o'clock in the afternoon the 19th Brigade under General Drummond arrived from Valenciennes and took up a position on the extreme left of our front, extending the line of the 5th Division as far as Condé itself, on the outskirts of which town were the 1st Cameronians, with the 2nd Middlesex on their right, and the 2nd R. Welsh Fusiliers again beyond.

They were hardly in position before the action became general all along the line of the canal.

The most serious attack in this quarter was on the bridge at Les Herbières, held by the 2nd K.O.S.B. This regiment had thrown one company forward on the north side, along the Pommeroeul road, with the remaining companies lining the south bank of the canal, and the machine-guns dominating the situation on the north side of the canal from the top storey of the highest house on the south side. The dispositions for defence were good, but on the other hand the K.O.S.B. were throughout the action a good deal harassed by a thick wood running up close to the north bank, in which the Germans were able to concentrate without coming under observation. Several times their infantry were seen massing on the edge of this wood with a view to a charge, but on each occasion the attack died away under the rifle fire from the Pommeroeul road and canal bank, and the machine-gun fire from the tall house beyond.

In the meanwhile, though undoubtedly inflicting very heavy losses on the enemy, the K.O.S.B. were losing men all the time, Captain Spencer, Captain Kennedy and Major Chandos-Leigh being early among the casualties. Curiously enough, the machine-gun position, though sufficiently conspicuous, was not located by the enemy for some considerable time, but eventually it became the object of much attention. In the end, however, it was luckily able to withdraw without loss, being more fortunate in this respect than the machine-gun section of the K.O.Y.L.I. on the right under Lieutenant Pepys, that officer being the first man killed in action in the battalion, if not in the whole division.

The Germans, in spite of all efforts, were able to make no material headway along the straight canal, nor was the advantage of the fighting in that quarter by any means on their side, but with the abandonment of the Nimy salient the withdrawal of the troops to the left of it became imperative, for reasons already explained, and in the evening the 5th Division received the order to retire. This was not till long after the 3rd Division had abandoned the Nimy salient. The three brigades of this latter division, after putting up a heroic defence and suffering very severe casualties, got the order to retire at 3 p.m., whereupon the R. Fusiliers fell slowly back through Mons to Hyon, and the R. Scots Fusiliers, who had put up a great fight at Jemappes, through Flénu. The blowing up of the Jemappes bridge gave a lot of trouble. Corporal Jarvis, R.E., worked at it for one and a half hours, continuously under fire, before he eventually managed to get it destroyed under the very noses of the Germans. He got a private of the R. Scots Fusiliers, named Heron, to help him, who got the D.C.M. Jarvis got the Victoria Cross.

The retirement of the R. Fusiliers from their dangerous position along the western boundary of the salient was not an easy matter. Before cover could be got they had to cross 250 yards of flat open ground swept at very close range by shrapnel and machine-gun fire. Dease had now been hit five times and was quite unable to move. Lieutenant Steele, who was the only man in the whole section who had not been killed or wounded, caught him up in his arms and carried him across the fire zone to a place of safety beyond, where however he later on succumbed to his wounds. Dease was posthumously awarded the Victoria Cross, as also was Private Godley for his machine-gun work on the Ghlin bridge.

The 9th Brigade after abandoning the salient remained in the open fields near the Mons hospital till two o'clock in the morning, when it continued its retirement towards Frameries. The wounded were left in the Mons hospital. At Flénu the R. Scots

Fusiliers lingered rather too long, and were caught near the railway junction by some very mobile machine-guns, which caused a number of casualties, Captain Rose being killed, and several other officers wounded.

By dusk the new line running through Montreuil, Boussu, Wasmes, Paturages and Frameries had been taken up by the greater part of the 2nd A.C., but the two extremities, *i.e.*, the 14th, 15th and 19th Brigades on the left and the 8th Brigade on the right, remained in their original positions till the middle of the night. The latter brigade then retired through Nouvelles and Quévy to Amfroipret, just beyond Bavai, where it bivouacked. This brigade in common with the 9th Brigade had suffered very severely, the Middlesex alone having lost 15 officers and 353 rank and file.

By night the Germans had completed their pontoon bridges across the canal, and it became evident that they were advancing in great force in the direction of Frameries, Paturages and Wasmes. Sir Horace realized that the 3rd Division had been too severely knocked about during the day to hold the position unaided for long against the weight of troops known to be advancing. He accordingly motored over to the C. in C. to ask for the loan of the 5th Brigade which was at Bougnies, four miles off, and on the main road to Frameries. This was readily granted him, and without delay the 5th Brigade set out, half of it remaining in Frameries, and the other half passing on to Paturages.

In the meanwhile, however, came a most unwelcome change of programme. The first line in the Mons salient had been obviously untenable for long, and had been recognized as such by our commanders, but the line now held was a different matter altogether, and there was every reasonable expectation that it could be successfully defended, at any rate for a very considerable time. At 2 a.m., however, Sir Horace received the order to abandon it and retire without delay to the Valenciennes to Maubeuge road, as the French on our right were retreating. Not only was this unexpected order highly distasteful to the soldier-spirit of the corps, but it involved difficulties of a grave nature with regard to the clearance of the transport and impedimenta generally, and severe and costly rear-guard actions seemed inevitable. At Paturages the Oxfordshire L.I. from the newly-arrived 5th Brigade was detailed for this duty, and dug itself in in rear of the town, while the 3rd Division continued its retirement to Bermeries. The Germans, however, contented themselves with shelling and then occupying the town, and made no attempt to follow through on the far side—a matter for pronounced congratulation, the position of the 5th Brigade being very bad and its line of retreat worse. It is to be supposed that the attractions of the town were for the moment stronger than the lust of battle. There also can be no question but that the Germans lost very heavily in their advance on Frameries and Paturages, the British shrapnel being beautifully timed, and knocking the attacking columns to pieces.

At noon the 5th Brigade returned to its own division at Bavai, the 23rd Brigade R.F.A. remaining behind at Paturages to give all the exits from the town an hour's bombardment, in case the German pursuit might become too pressing.

In the cobbled streets of Bavai a fine confusion was found to reign—companies without regiments and officers without companies, and various units mixed up anyhow. The Staff officers had their hands very full.

In the meantime, while Frameries and Paturages were being occupied by the enemy with little or no infantry opposition, and with little attempt on the part of the enemy at further pursuit, the market square at Wasmes presented a very different scene. This town had been shelled from daybreak, the enemy's fire being replied to with magnificent courage and with the most conspicuous success by a single howitzer battery standing out by itself half a mile from the town. An officer, perched on the top of one of the huge slag heaps with which the country is dotted, was able to direct operations with the highest degree of accuracy, and rendered services to the retreating force which are beyond estimation.

At ten o'clock the German infantry attacked the town with the utmost confidence, advancing through the narrow streets in close column. A certain surprise, however, awaited them. In the town, lining the market square and the streets to either side, were the K.O.Y.L.I., the R. West Kents, the Bedfords and the Duke of Wellington's Regiment, these regiments having been detailed for rear-guard work and having successfully withstood the bombardment. The heads of the German columns, the moment they appeared in sight, were met by a concentrated rifle and machine-gun fire and were literally mown down like grass. Their losses were enormous. Time after time they were driven back, and time after time they advanced again with splendid but useless courage. After two hours' fighting in the streets, during which the enemy was able to make no headway, our troops, having fulfilled their duty as rear-guard, were able to withdraw in good order to St. Vaast, which was reached at dusk. The losses on our side were heavy. The R. West Kents alone had Major Pack-Beresford, Captain Philips, and Lieutenants Sewell and Broadwood killed, and several other officers wounded. The Duke of Wellington's also lost heavily. Sergeant Spence of that regiment distinguished himself very greatly. During one of the German advances he was badly wounded, but ignoring his wounds he charged with a platoon down one of the narrow streets to the right of the square, and drove the enemy clean out of the town with great loss. He was awarded the D.C.M. as was also Sergeant Hunt of the Bedfords.

Further west, at the extreme left of our line, the retirement was effected with even greater difficulty than at Wasmes. The second line of defence through Montreuil, Boussu, Wasmes, Paturages and Frameries—which in effect merely constituted a change of front with the right thrown half back—of necessity left the western end of our line in close proximity to the enemy's advance. In other words, the further west the greater the difficulty of retiring on account of the closer presence of the enemy. The 14th, 15th and 19th Brigades, with a view to conforming to the general direction of the second line of defence, had remained north of the Valenciennes—Mons road and railway throughout the night of the 23rd. In the morning, when the order to retire to the Valenciennes road came, the 15th and 19th Brigades crossed the railway at Quiverain, and the 14th at Thulin, but by this time the enemy was close upon their heels. The 1st Cavalry Division was able to help their retirement to a certain extent by dismounting and lining the railway embankment, from which position they got the advancing Germans in half flank, and did considerable execution. By 11.30, however, they too had been forced to retire to Andregnies. An urgent message now arrived from Sir Charles Fergusson, commanding the 5th Division, saying that he could not possibly extricate his division unless prompt and effective help was given by the cavalry. On receiving this message, General de Lisle, who was at Andregnies, sent off the 18th Hussars to the high ground along the Quiverain to Eloges road with orders to there dismount and make the most of the ground. The 119th Battery R.F.A. was at this time just south-west of Eloges, and L Battery R.H.A. just north-east of Andregnies, both being on the main road to Angre and about three miles apart. The 4th Dragoon Guards and 9th Lancers were in Andregnies itself.

No sooner were his dispositions made than the German columns were seen advancing from the direction of Quiverain towards Andregnies. De Lisle told the two regiments in the village that they had got to stop the advance at all costs, even if it entailed a charge. The very suggestion of a charge never fails to act as a tonic to any British cavalry regiment, and in great elation of spirits the two cavalry regiments debouched from the village, the 4th Dragoon Guards making their exit from the left, and the two squadrons of the 9th Lancers from the right.

The enemy were now seen some 2,000 yards away, the intervening ground being mainly stubble fields in which the corn stooks were still standing. The Germans no sooner saw the cavalry advancing with the evident intention of charging than they scattered in every direction, taking shelter behind the corn stooks and any other cover that presented itself, and opening fire from these positions. The cavalry advanced in the most perfect order, and was on the point of making a final charge when it became evident that this was impossible owing to a wire fence which divided two of the stubble fields.

With great coolness and presence of mind, the two C.Os, Colonel Mullens of the 4th Dragoon Guards, and Colonel Campbell of the 9th Lancers, without pausing, wheeled their troops to the right, and took cover behind some big slag heaps, where they dismounted under shelter. From this position the cavalry opened a galling fire on the advancing Germans, the two batteries on the Angre road joining in. The original scheme of charging the enemy having been frustrated, it now became necessary to get fresh orders from headquarters, and Colonel Campbell accordingly galloped back across the open, in full view of the enemy and under a salute of bullets, to see the Brigadier, leaving Captain Lucas-Tooth in command of the two squadrons of the 9th Lancers.

For four hours the fight was kept up, the led horses being gradually withdrawn into safety, while the dismounted cavalry with their two attendant batteries held the enemy in check. During the whole of this period the Germans were quite unable to advance beyond the wire fence which had so suddenly changed a proposed charge into a dismounted attack. Captain Lucas-Tooth was awarded the D.S.O. for the gallantry with which he conducted this defence, and for the great coolness and skill with which he withdrew his men and horses.

General de Lisle's object having now been achieved, the dismounted men were gradually withdrawn. During the course of one of these withdrawals, Captain Francis Grenfell, 9th Lancers, noticed Major Alexander of the 119th Battery in difficulties with regard to the withdrawal of his guns. All his horses had been killed, and almost every man in the detachment was either killed or wounded. Captain Grenfell offered assistance which was gladly accepted, and presently he returned with eleven officers of his regiment and some forty men. The ground was very heavy and the guns had to be run back by hand under a ceaseless fire, but they were all saved, Major Alexander, Captain Grenfell and the rest of the officers working as hard as the men. Captain Grenfell was already wounded when he arrived, and was again hit while manhandling one of the guns, but he declined to retire till they were all saved. For this fine performance, Major Alexander and Captain Grenfell[1] were each awarded the Victoria Cross, Sergeants Turner and Davids getting the D.C.M. Others no doubt merited it too, but where so many were deserving it was hard to discriminate.

We may now consider the retirement of the 2nd A.C. to the Valenciennes to Maubeuge road to have been successfully effected; and the fall of night saw this corps dotted at intervals along this road between Jerlain and Bavai.

---

1. Of this famous fighting family the twins Captain Rivy and Captain Francis Grenfell have both been killed during the present war. Their elder brother, R. S. Grenfell, was killed at Omdurman during the Egyptian campaign, and their cousin Claud Grenfell at Spion Kop, in the Boer war. Two other cousins, the Honourable J. Grenfell and Honourable G. Grenfell, have also fallen in the present war. Lieutenant-Colonel Cecil Grenfell, a brother of the twins, is at the moment of writing fighting in the Dardanelles.

While they are there, enjoying their few hours' respite from marching and fighting, it may be well to cast a retrospective glance at the doings of the 1st A.C. This corps had so far had little serious fighting, but it had been very far from inactive, and in point of fact, it had probably covered more ground in the way of marching and counter-marching than its partner, owing to repeated scares of enemy attacks which did not materialize. At daybreak on the 24th, the 2nd Division was ordered to make a demonstration in the direction of Binche with a view to diverting attention from the retirement of the 2nd A.C. The 2nd Division now consisted of the 4th and 6th Brigades only, the 5th Brigade having, as we know, gone to Frameries and Paturages to help the 3rd Division. These two brigades, then, advanced at daybreak in the direction of Binche to the accompaniment of a tremendous cannonade, in which the artillery of the 1st Division joined from the neighbourhood of Pleissant. There was a great noise and a vigorous artillery response from the enemy, but not much else, and after an hour or so the 2nd Division returned to the Mons—Maubeuge road, where it entrenched. Here it remained for some four hours, when it retired to the Quévy road and again entrenched. Nothing, however, in the way of a serious attack occurred, and at five o'clock in the evening it fell back to its appointed place just east of Bavai. The 1st Division shortly afterwards arrived at Feignies and Longueville, and the whole British Army was once more in line between Jerlain and Maubeuge, with Bavai as the dividing point between the two A.Cs.

CHAPTER 3

The Retreat From Mons

In modern warfare the boundary line between the words "victory" and "defeat" is not easy to fix. It is perhaps particularly difficult to fix in relation to the part played by any arbitrarily selected group of regiments; the fact being that the value of results achieved can only be truly gauged from the standpoint of their conformity with the general scheme. So thoroughly is this now understood that the word "victory" or "defeat" is seldom used by either side in connection with individual actions, except in relation to the strategical bearing of such actions on the ultimate aims of the war council.

The name of Mons will always be associated in the public mind with the idea of retreat, and retreat is the traditional companion of defeat. Incidentally, too, retreat is bitterly distasteful both to the soldier and the onlooking public. It must be borne in mind, however, that retreat is a more difficult operation than advance, and that when a retreat is achieved with practically intact forces, capable of an immediate advance when called upon, and capable of making considerable captures of guns and prisoners in the process of advance, a great deal of hesitation is needed before the word "defeat" can be definitely associated with such results.

During the first three months of the war the general idea on both sides was to stretch out seawards, and so overlap the western flank of the opposing army. At the moment of the arrival of the British force on the Belgian frontier, Germany had outstripped France in this race to the west, and there was a very real danger of the French army being outflanked; so much so, in fact, that in order to avoid any such calamity, a rearrangement of the French pieces seemed called for, to the necessary prejudice of the general scheme. However, at the psychological moment, the much-discussed British Force materialized and became a live obstacle in the path of the German outflanking movement. Its allotted task was to baulk this movement, while the French combination in rear was being smoothly unfolded.

It is now a matter of history that this was done. The German outflanking movement failed; Von Kluck's right wing was held in check; and the British Force fell back unbroken and fighting all the way, while the French dispositions further south and west were systematically and securely shaping for success.

Was Mons, then, a defeat? For forty-eight hours the British had held up the German forces north of the Maubeuge—Valenciennes road; the left of the French army had been effectively protected, and—over and above all—the British force had succeeded in retiring in perfect order and intact, except for the ordinary wear and tear of battle. It had "done its job;" it had accomplished the exact purpose for which it had been put in the field, and it had withdrawn thirty-five miles, or thereabouts, to face about and repeat the operation.

In attaching the label to such a performance, neither "victory" nor "defeat" is a word that quite fits. Such crude classifications are relics of primordial standards when scalps and loot were the only recognized marks of victory. Today, generals commanding armies rather search for honour in the field of duty—duty accomplished, orders obeyed. These simple formulae have always been the watchwords of the soldier-unit, whether that unit be a man, a platoon, a company or a regiment. Now, with the limitless increase in the size of armaments, a unit may well be an army corps, or even a combination of army corps, and the highest aim of the general officer commanding such a unit must be—as of old—fulfilment of duty, obedience to orders.

To the Briton, then, dwelling in mind on the battle of Mons, the reflection will always come with a certain pleasant flavour that the British army was a unit which "did its job," and did it in a way worthy of the highest British traditions. More than this it is not open to man—whether military or civilian—to do.

Map showing the first seven days of the retreat from Mons, with the routes followed by each Division. The dates given refer to the nights during which the troops rested, the days being spent in marching.

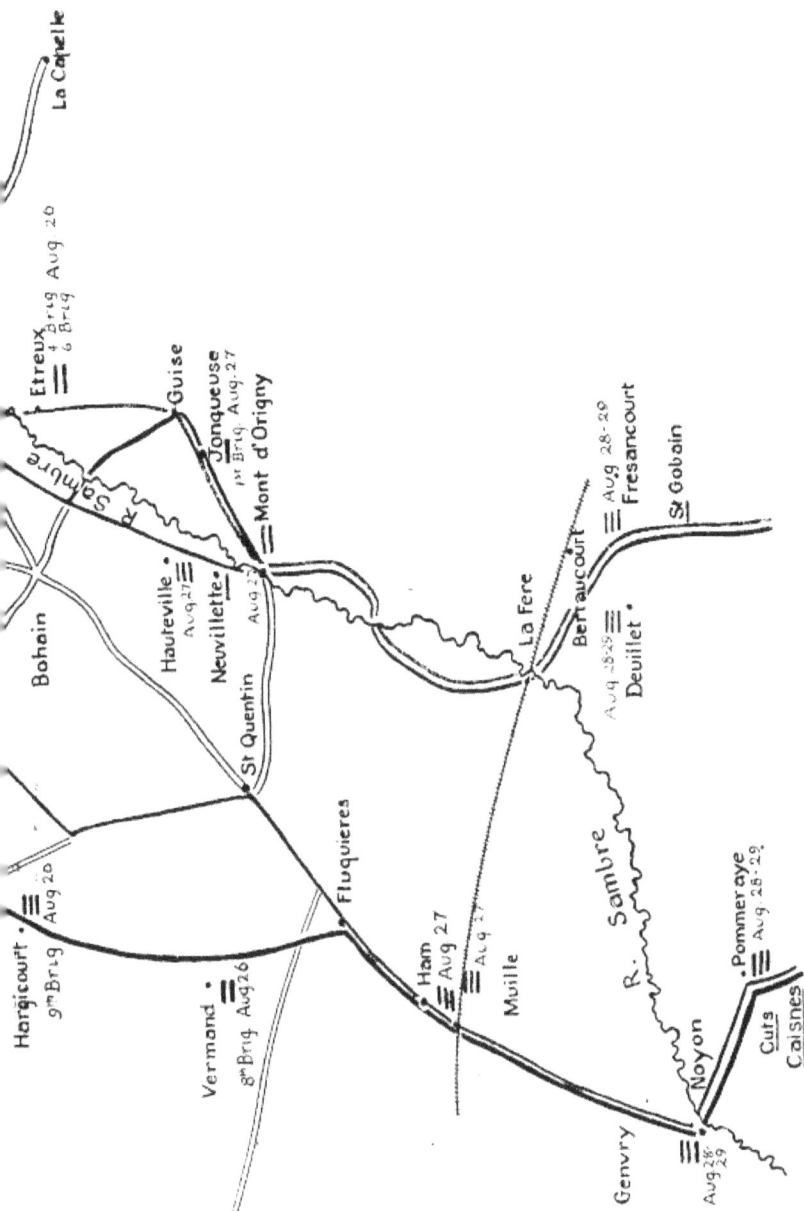

La Capelle

Etreux 4 Brig Aug 26
6 Brig

Guise

Jonqueuse 1st Brig Aug 27

Mont d'Origny

R. Sambre

Bohain

Hauteville Aug 27
Neuvillette Aug 27

St Quentin

Hargicourt 9th Brig Aug 26

Vermond 8th Brig Aug 26

Fluquieres

Ham Aug 27

Muille Aug 27

Genvry Aug 28-29

Noyon

R. Sambre

La Fere

Bertaucourt Aug 28-29
Fresancourt

St Gobain

Deuillet Aug 28-29

Pommeraye Aug 28-29

Cuts
Caisnes

The British army continued its retreat from the Maubeuge road in the early morning of the 25th. The original intention of the C. in C. had been to make a stand along this road. That, however, was when the numbers opposed to him were supposed to be very much less than they ultimately turned out to be. Now it was known that there were three army corps on his heels, to say nothing of an additional flanking corps that was said to be working up from the direction of Tournai. This last was quite an ugly factor in the case, as it opened the possibility of the little British force being hemmed in against Maubeuge and surrounded. The road system to the rear, too, was sketchy, and by no means well adapted to a hurried retreat—especially east of Bavai; nor was the country itself suitable for defence, the standing crops greatly limiting the field of fire. All things considered, it was decided not to fight here, but to get back to the Cambrai to Le Cateau road, and make that the next line of resistance.

Accordingly, about four o'clock on the morning of the 25th, the whole army turned its face southward once more. The 5th Division, which during the process of retirement had geographically changed places with the 3rd Division, travelled by the mathematically straight Roman road which runs to Le Cateau, along the western edge of the Forêt de Mormal, while the 3rd Division took the still more western route by Le Quesnoy and Solesme, their retreat being effectively covered by the 1st and 3rd C.B. At Le Quesnoy the cavalry, thinking that the enemy's attentions were becoming too pressing, dismounted and lined the railway embankment, which offered fine cover for men and horses. From here the Germans could be plainly seen advancing diagonally across the fields in innumerable short lines, which the cavalry fire was able to enfilade and materially check.

In the meanwhile the 1st A.C., which had throughout formed the eastern wing of the army, had perforce to put up with the eastern line of retreat on the far side of the Forêt de Mormal, a circumstance which—owing to the longer and more roundabout nature of the route followed—was not without its effect on the subsequent battle of Le Cateau. The six brigades belonging to the last named corps started at all hours of the morning between 4 and 8.30, at which latter hour the 2nd Brigade—the last to leave—

quitted its billets at Feignies and marched to Marbaix. The 1st Brigade went to Taisnières, the 4th to Landrecies, the 6th to Maroilles, while the 5th got no farther than Leval, having had a scare and a consequent set-back at Pont-sur-Sambre.

Here then we may leave the 1st A.C. on the night of the 25th, considerably scattered, and separated by distances varying from ten to thirty miles from its partner, which was at the time making preparations to put up a fight along the Cambrai—Le Cateau road.

The original scheme agreed between the C. in C. and his two army corps commanders, had been that the 2nd Division should pass on westward across the river at Landrecies and link up with the 5th Division at Le Cateau, blowing up behind it the bridges at Landrecies and Catillon. This scheme was upset by the activity of the enemy on the east side of the Forêt de Mormal, rear-guard actions being forced upon each of the three divisional brigades at Pont-sur-Sambre, Landrecies and Maroilles respectively. These rear-guard actions, coupled with the longer and worse roads they had to follow, in the end so seriously delayed the retirement of the 2nd Division as to entirely put out of court any question of their co-operation with the 2nd A.C. at Le Cateau on the 26th.

The 4th Brigade got the nearest at Landrecies, but it got there dead beat and then had to fight all night. The 1st Division was a good thirty miles off at Marbaix and Taisnières, where it had its hands sufficiently full with its own affairs. This division may, therefore, for the moment, be put aside as a negligible quantity in the very critical situation which was developing west of the Sambre. The movements of the 2nd Division were not only more eventful in themselves, but were of far greater practical interest to the commander of the 2nd A.C. in his endeavour to successfully withdraw his harassed Mons army. We may, therefore, follow this division in rather closer detail during the day and night of the 25th.

In reckoning the miscarriage of the arrangements originally planned, it must not be lost sight of that the march from the Bavai road to the Le Cateau road was the longest to be accomplished during the retreat. From Bavai to Le Cateau is twenty-two miles as the crow flies. It is probable that the 5th Division, following the straight Roman road, did not greatly exceed this distance, but to the route of the 3rd Division it is certainly necessary to add another five miles, and to that of the 2nd Division, ten. In reflecting that the pursuing Germans had to cover the same distance, the following facts must be borne in mind. The training of our military schools has always been based to a very great extent on the experience of the previous war. The equipment of our military ménage is also largely designed to meet the exigencies of a war on somewhat similar lines to that of the last. Our wars for sixty years past have been "little wars" fought in far-off countries more or less uncivilized; and the probability of our armies fighting on European soil has always been considered as remote. Germany, on the other hand, has had few "little wars," but has, on the other hand, for many years been preparing for the contingency of a war amidst European surroundings. As a consequence, her army equipment at the outbreak of war was constructed primarily with a view to rapid movements on paved and macadamized roads; certainly ours was not. The German advance was therefore assisted by every known device for facilitating the rapid movement of troops along the roads of modern civilization. Later on, by requisitioning the motor-lorries and vans of trading firms, we placed ourselves on more or less of an equal footing in this respect, but that was not when the necessity for rapid movement was most keenly felt. The Germans reaped a double advantage, for not only were they capable of quicker movement, but they were also able to overtake our rear-guards with troops that were not jaded with interminable marching.

It must also be borne in mind that a pursuing force marches straight to its objective with a minimum of exhaustion in relation to the work accomplished, an advantage which certainly cannot be claimed for a retreating force which has to turn and fight.

We may now return to the 2nd Division, setting out from La Longueville on its stupendous undertaking. At first the whole division followed the one road by the eastern edge of the Forêt de Mormal, the impedimenta in front, the troops plodding behind. This road was choked from end to end with refugees and their belongings, chiefly from Maubeuge and district, and the average pace of the procession was about two miles an hour. An order came to hurry up so that the bridges over the Sambre could be blown up before the Germans came; but it was waste of breath. The troops were dead beat. Though they had so far had no fighting, they had done a terrible amount of marching, counter-marching and digging during the past four days, and they were dead beat. The reservists' boots were all too small, and their feet swelled horribly. Hundreds fell out from absolute exhaustion. The worst cases were taken along in the transport wagons; the rest became stragglers, following along behind as best they were able. Some of the cavalry that saw them pass said that their eyes were fixed in a ghastly stare, and they stumbled along like blind men. At Leval the division split up, the 4th Brigade taking the road to Landrecies, and the 6th that to Maroilles. The 5th Brigade, which was doing rear-guard to the division, got no farther than Leval, where it prepared to put up a fight along the railway line; for there was a scare that the Germans were very close behind. The Oxfordshire Light Infantry were even sent back along the road they had already travelled to Pont-sur-Sambre, where they entrenched. The Germans, however, did not come.

CHAPTER 4

The Fight at Landrecies

The 4th (Guards') Brigade reached Landrecies at 1 p.m. This brigade had made the furthest progress towards the contemplated junction with the 2nd A.C., and they were very tired. They went into billets at once, some in the barracks, some in the town. They had about four hours' rest; then there came an alarm that the Germans were advancing on the town, and the brigade got to its feet. The four battalions were split up into companies—one to each of the exits from the town. The Grenadiers were on the western side; the 2nd Coldstream on the south and east; and the 3rd Coldstream to the north and north-west. The Irish Guards saw to the barricading of the streets with transport wagons and such-like obstacles. They also loop-holed the end houses of the streets facing the country.

As a matter of fact the attack did not take place till 8.30 p.m., and then it was entirely borne by two companies of the 3rd Battalion Coldstream Guards. At the north-west angle of the town there is a narrow street, known as the Faubourg Soyère. Two hundred yards from the town this branches out into two roads, each leading into the Forêt de Mormal. Here, at the junction of the roads, the Hon. A. Monck's company had been stationed. The sky was very overcast, and the darkness fell early. Shortly after 8.30 p.m. infantry was heard advancing from the direction of the forest; they were singing French songs, and a flashlight turned upon the head of the column showed up French uniforms. It was not till they were practically at arms' length that a second flashlight detected the German uniforms in rear of the leading sections. The machine-gun had no time to speak before the man in charge was bayoneted and the gun itself captured. A hand-to-hand fight in the dark followed, in which revolvers and bayonets played the principal part, the Coldstream being gradually forced back by weight of numbers towards the entrance to the town. Here Captain Longueville's company was in reserve in the Faubourg Soyère itself, and through a heavy fire he rushed up his men to the support of Captain Monck.

The arrival of the reserve company made things rather more level as regards numbers, though—as it afterwards transpired—the Germans were throughout in a majority of at least two to one. Colonel Feilding and Major Matheson now arrived on the spot, and took over control. Inspired by their presence and example, the two Coldstream companies now attacked their assailants with great vigour and drove them back with considerable loss into the shadows of the forest. From here the Germans trained a light field-gun on to the mouth of the Faubourg Soyère, and, firing shrapnel and star-shell at point-blank range, made things very unpleasant for the defenders. Flames began to shoot up from a wooden barn at the end of the street, but were quickly got under, with much promptitude and courage, by a private of the name of Wyatt, who twice extinguished them under a heavy fire. A blaze of light at this point would have been fatal to the safety of the defenders, and Wyatt, whose act was one involving great personal danger, was subsequently awarded the Victoria Cross for this act, and for the conspicuous bravery which he displayed a week later when wounded at Villers-Cotteret.

In the meanwhile Colonel Feilding had sent off for a how-itzer, which duly arrived and was aimed at the flash of the German gun. By an extraordinary piece of marksmanship, or of luck, as the case may be, the third shot got it full and the field-gun ceased from troubling. The German infantry thereupon renewed their attack, but failed to make any further headway during the night, and in the end went off in their motor-lorries, taking their wounded with them.

It turned out that the attacking force, consisting of a battalion of 1,200 men, with one light field-piece, had been sent on in these lorries in advance of the general pursuit, with the idea of seizing Landrecies and its important bridge before the British could arrive and link up with the 2nd A.C. The attack *quâ* attack failed conspicuously, inasmuch as the enemy was driven back with very heavy loss; but it is possible that it accomplished its purpose in helping to prevent the junction of the two A.Cs. This, however, is in a region of speculation, which it is profitless to pursue further.

The Landrecies fight lasted six hours and was a very brilliant little victory for the 3rd Coldstream; but it was expensive. Lord Hawarden and the Hon. A. Windsor-Clive were killed, and Captain Whitehead, Lieutenant Keppel and Lieutenant Rowley were wounded. The casualties among the rank and file amounted to 170, of whom 153 were left in the hospital at Landrecies. The two companies engaged fought under particularly trying conditions, and many of the rank and file showed great gallantry. Conspicuous amongst these were Sergeant Fox and Private Thomas, each of whom was awarded the D.C.M. The German losses were, of course, unascertainable, but they were undoubtedly very much higher than ours.

At 3.30 a.m. on the 26th, just as the 2nd A.C. in their trenches ten miles away to the west were beginning to look northward for the enemy, the 4th Brigade left Landrecies and continued its retirement down the beautiful valley of the Sambre.

Chapter 5

Maroilles

On the same night the town of Maroilles further east was the scene of another little fight. About 10 p.m. a report arrived that the main German column was advancing on the bridge over the Petit Helpe and that the squadron of the 15th Hussars which had been left to guard the bridge was insufficient for the purpose. The obstruction of this bridge was a matter of the very first importance, as its passage would have opened up a short cut for the Germans, by which they might easily have cut off the 4th Brigade south of Landrecies. Accordingly the 1st Berks were ordered off back along the road they had already travelled to hold the position at all costs. The ground near the bridge here is very swampy, and the only two approaches are by means of raised causeways, one of which faces the bridge, while the other lies at right angles. Along this latter the Berks crept up, led by Colonel Graham.

The night was intensely dark, and the causeway very narrow, and bounded on each side by a deep fosse, into which many of the men slipped. The Germans, as it turned out, had already forced the bridge, and were in the act of advancing along the causeway; and in the pitch blackness of the night the two forces suddenly bumped one into the other. Neither side had fixed bayonets, for fear of accidents in the dark, and in the scrimmage which followed it was chiefly a case of rifle-butts and fists. At this game the Germans proved no match for our men, and were gradually forced back to the bridge-head, where they were held for the remainder of the night.

In the small hours of the morning the Germans, who turned

out not to be the main column, but only a strong detachment, threw up the sponge and withdrew westward towards the Sambre, following the right bank of the Petit Helpe. Whereupon the 1st Berks—having achieved their purpose—followed the rest of the 2nd Division along the road to Etreux.

CHAPTER 6

The Le Cateau Problem

It is necessary now to cast a momentary eye upon the general situation of the British forces on the night of August 25th. The 3rd and 5th Divisions, in spite of the severe fighting of the 23rd and 24th, and in spite of great exhaustion, had successfully accomplished the arduous march to the Le Cateau position. The 19th Brigade and the 4th Division, the latter fresh from England, were already there, extending the selected line towards the west. So far, so good. The 1st and 2nd Divisions, however, owing to causes which have already been explained, were not in a position to co-operate; and it was clear that, if battle was to be offered at Le Cateau, the already battered 2nd A.C. (supplemented by the newly-arrived troops) would have to stand the shock single-handed.

A consideration of these facts induced the C. in C. to change his original intention of making a stand behind the Le Cateau road, and he decided to continue his retirement to the single line of rail which runs from St. Quentin to Roisel, where his force would be once more in line. This change of plan he communicated to his two Army Corps commanders, Sir Douglas Haig and Sir Horace Smith-Dorrien. The former fell in with it gladly; the latter, however, was not to the same extent a free agent, and he returned word that, in view of the immense superiority in numbers of the German forces, which were practically treading on his heels, and of the necessarily slow progress made by his tired troops, it was impossible to continue his retirement, and that he had no alternative but to turn and fight. To which the C. in C. replied that he must do the best he could, but that he could give him no support from the 1st A.C., that corps being effectively cut off by natural obstacles from the scene of action. As a matter of fact the 1st Division was a good thirty miles away to the east at Marbaix and Taisnières. The 2nd Division was nearer, but very much scattered, the 5th Brigade—owing to rear-guard scares—being still twenty miles behind at Leval, and quite out of the reckoning, as far as the impending battle was concerned. The 4th Brigade, on the other hand, in spite of its all-night fight at Landrecies, might, by super-human efforts, have crossed the Sambre during the night at the little village of Ors, and reached the flank of the Le Cateau battlefield towards eight on the following morning; but the wisdom of such a move would have been more than questionable in view of the complete exhaustion of the troops, and, in point of fact, no such order reached the brigade. The orders were to fall back on St. Quentin, and by the time the first shot was fired at Le Cateau, the brigade was well on its way to Etreux.

Four miles further east, at Maroilles, the order to retire raised some doubts and a certain difference of opinion among the various commanders of the 6th Brigade as to the best route to be followed in order to arrive at the St. Quentin position. Local opinion was divided, and, in the end, the commanders assembled at midnight in the cemetery to decide the point, with the result that it was arranged that each C.O. should follow the road that seemed best to him.

It will be seen then that the disposition of the 1st A.C. was such that the C. in C. by no means overstated the case when he told Sir Horace that he could give him no help from that quarter. The position of the 2nd A.C. was now very nearly desperate, and it is to be doubted whether Sir Horace or the C. in C. himself saw the dawn break on August 26th with any real hope at heart that the three divisions west of the Sambre could be saved from capture or annihilation.

On paper the extrication of Sir Horace's force seemed in truth an impossibility. Three British divisions, very imperfectly entrenched, were awaiting the onset of seven German divisions, flushed with uninterrupted victory, and backed up by an over-whelming preponderance in artillery. Both flanks of the British force were practically in the air, the only protection on the right being the 1st and 3rd C.B. at Le Souplet, and on the left Allenby with another two cavalry brigades at Seranvillers. As a buffer against the German army corps which was threatening the British flank from Tournai, two Cavalry Brigades were clearly a negligible quantity. Desperate diseases call for desperate remedies, and the C. in C. had recourse to the only expedient in which lay a hope of salvation from the threatened flank attack, should it come. General Sordet was at Avesnes with three divisions of French cavalry, and the C. in C.—with all the persuasion possible—put the urgency of the situation before him. The railways were no help; they ran all wrong; cavalry alone could save the situation; would he go? General Sordet—with the permission of his chief—went. It was a forty mile march, and cavalry horses were none too fresh in those days. Still he went, and in the end did great and gallant work; but not on the morning of the 26th. On that fateful day— or at least on the morning of that fateful day—his horses were ridden to a standstill, and he could do nothing.

Chapter 7

Le Cateau

The battle of August 26th is loosely spoken of as the Cambrai—
Le Cateau battle, but, as a matter of fact, the British troops were
never within half a dozen miles of Cambrai, nor, for that matter, were they actually at Le Cateau itself. The 5th Division on
the right reached from a point halfway between Le Cateau and
Reumont to Troisvilles, the 15th Brigade, which was its left-hand
brigade, being just east of that place. Then came the three brigades
of the 3rd Division, the 9th Brigade being north of Troisvilles, the
8th Brigade on the left of it north of Audencourt, with the 7th
Brigade curled round the northern side of Caudry in the form of a
horseshoe. Beyond was the 4th Division at Hautcourt. The whole
frontage covered about eight miles, and for half that distance ran
along north of the Cambrai to St. Quentin railway.

The 4th Division, under General Snow, had just arrived from
England; and these fresh troops were already in position when the
Mons army straggled in on the night of the 25th and was told off
to its various allotted posts by busy staff officers. The allotted posts
did not turn out to be all that had been hoped for. Trenches, it is
true, had been prepared (dug by French woman labour!), but many
faced the wrong way, and all were too short. The short ones could
be lengthened, but the others had to be redug. The men were
dead beat: the ground baked hard, and there were no entrenching
tools—these having long ago been thrown away. Picks were got
from the farms and the men set to work as best they could, but of
shovels there were practically none, and in the majority of cases the
men scooped up the loosened earth with mess-tins and with their

hands. The result was, trenches by courtesy, but poor things to stand between tired troops and the terrific artillery fire to which they were presently to be subjected.

The battle of Le Cateau was in the main an artillery duel, and a very unequal one at that. The afternoon infantry attack was only sustained by certain devoted regiments who failed to interpret with sufficient readiness the order to retire. Some of these regiments—as the price of their ignorance of how to turn their backs to the foe—were all but annihilated. But this is a later story. Up to midday the battle was a mere artillery duel. Our infantry lined their inadequate trenches and were bombarded for some half a dozen hours on end. Our artillery replied with inconceivable heroism, but they were outnumbered by at least five to one. They also—perhaps with wisdom—directed their fire more at the infantry than at the opposing batteries. The former could be plainly seen massing in great numbers on the crest of the ridge some two thousand yards away, and advancing in a succession of lines down the slope to the hidden ground below. They presented a tempting target, and their losses from our shrapnel must have been enormous. By the afternoon, however, many of our batteries had been silenced, and the German gunners had it more or less their own way. The sides were too unequal. Our infantry then became mere targets—*Kanonen Futter*. It was an ordeal of the most trying description conceivable, and one which can only arise where the artillery of one side is hopelessly outnumbered by that of the other; and it is to be doubted whether any other troops in the world would have stood it as long as did the 2nd A.C. at Le Cateau. The enemy's bombardment was kept up till midday. Then it slackened off so as to allow of the further advance of their infantry, who by this time had pushed forward into the concealment of the low ground, just north of the main road. By this time some of the 5th Division had begun to dribble away. That awful gun fire, to which our batteries were no longer able to reply, coupled with the insufficient trenches, was too much for human endurance. Sir Charles Fergusson, the Divisional General, with an absolute disregard of personal danger, galloped about among the bursting shells exhorting the division to stand fast. An eye-witness said that his survival through the day was nothing short of a miracle. It was a day indeed when the entire Staff from end to end of the line worked with an indefatigable heroism which could not be surpassed. In the 19th Brigade, for instance, Captain Jack, 1st Cameronians, was the sole survivor of the Brigade Staff at the end of the day, and this was through no fault of his. While supervising the retirement of the Argyll and Sutherlands, he coolly walked up and down the firing line without a vestige of protection, but by some curious law of chances was not hit. He was awarded a French decoration.

In spite of all, however, by 2.30 p.m., the right flank of the 5th Division had been turned, the enemy pressing forward into the gap between the two Army Corps, and Sir Charles sent word that the Division could hold its ground no longer. Sir Horace sent up all the available reserves he had, *viz.*, the 1st Cameronians and 2nd R. Welsh Fusiliers from the 19th Brigade, together with a battery, and these helped matters to some extent, but the immense numerical superiority of the enemy made anything in the nature of a prolonged stand impossible, and at 3 p.m. he ordered a general retirement. This was carried out in fairly good order by the 3rd and 4th Divisions, which had been less heavily attacked. The withdrawal of the 5th Division was more irregular, and the regiments which stuck it to the end—becoming practically isolated by the withdrawal of other units to right and left—suffered very severely.

This irregularity in retirement was noticeable all along the battle-front, some battalions grasping the meaning of the general order to retire with more readiness than others. Among those in the 5th Division who were slow to interpret the signal were the K.O.S.B. and the K.O.Y.L.I.

These two 13th Brigade battalions were next one another just north of Reumont, with the Manchester Regiment on the right of the K.O.Y.L.I. It was common talk among the men of the 5th Division that the French were coming up in support, and that, therefore, there must be no giving way. The French in question were—and only could be—General Sordet's cavalry, who, at the time, were plodding away in rear on their forty mile trek to the left flank of our army, and who could never under any circumstances have been of help to the 5th Division on the right of the Le Cateau battle-front. However, that was the rumour and they held on. Some of the K.O.S.B. in the first line trenches saw some men on their flank retiring, and, thinking it was a general order, followed suit. Colonel Stephenson personally re-conducted them back to their trenches. He was himself almost immediately afterwards knocked out by a shell; but the force of example had its effect, and there was no more retiring till the general order to that effect was unmistakable. This was about three o'clock. The final retirement of those battalions which had held on till the enemy was on the top of them was very difficult, and very costly in casualties, as they were mowed down by shrapnel and machine-gun fire the moment they left their trenches. It was during this retirement that Corporal Holmes, of the K.O.Y.L.I, won his Victoria Cross by picking up a wounded comrade and carrying him over a mile under heavy fire. Another Victoria Cross in the same battalion was won that day by Major Yate under very dramatic circumstances. His company had been in the second line of trenches during the bombardment, and had suffered terribly from the enemy's shell-fire directed at one of our batteries just behind. When the German infantry came swarming up in the afternoon, there were only nineteen sound men left in the company. These nineteen kept up their fire to the last moment and then left the trench and charged, headed by Major Yate. There could be but one result. Major Yate fell mortally wounded, and his gallant band of Yorkshiremen ceased to exist. It was the Thermopylae of B Company, 2nd K.O.Y.L.I. This battalion lost twenty officers and six hundred men during the battle, and was probably the heaviest sufferer in the 5th Division. It stuck it till the last moment and the enemy got round its right flank.

The 3rd Division line, further west, was also forced about three o'clock in the afternoon, when the enemy in great numbers broke through towards Troisvilles, to the right of the 9th Brigade, causing the whole division to retire. The actual order to retire in this case was passed down by word of mouth from right to left by galloping Staff officers, who—in the pandemonium that was reigning—were unable to get in touch with all the units of each battalion. As a result the retirement was necessarily irregular, and—as in the case of the 5th Division—the battalions that "stuck it" longest found themselves isolated and in time surrounded. This was the case with the 1st Gordon Highlanders, in the 8th Brigade, to whom the order to retire either never penetrated, or to whom it was too distasteful to be acted upon with promptitude. The exact circumstances of the annihilation of this historic battalion will never be known till the war is over, but the net result was that it lost 80 per cent. of its strength in killed, wounded and missing. The same fate overtook one company of the 2nd R. Scots in the same brigade. This company was practically wiped out and the battalion as a whole had some 400 casualties in killed and wounded. The whole division, in fact, suffered very severely in carrying out the retirement, the ground to the rear being very open and exposed, and the enemy's rifle and machine-gun fire incessant. The village of Audencourt had been heavily shelled all day and was a mass of blazing ruins, effectually barring any retirement by the high road, and forcing the retreating troops to take to the open country. Once, however, behind the railway, the retreat became more organized, and a series of small rear-guard fights were put up from behind the shelter of the embankment.

The 23rd Brigade R.F.A., under Colonel Butler, put in some most efficient work at this period, and materially assisted the retirement of the 8th Brigade. With remarkable coolness the gunners, entirely undisturbed by the general confusion reigning, continued to drop beautifully-timed shells among the advancing German infantry. The work of the artillery, in fact, all along the line was magnificent, and deeds of individual heroism were innumerable. The 37th Battery, for instance, kept up its shrapnel-fire on the advancing lines of Germans till these were within 300 yards of its position. Then Captain Reynolds, with some volunteer drivers, galloped up with two teams, and hitched them on to the two guns which had not been knocked out. Incredible as it may appear, in view of the hail of bullets directed at them, one of these guns was got safely away. The other was not. Captain Reynolds and Drivers Luke and Brain were given the Victoria Cross for this exploit. Sergeant Browne, of the same battery, got the D.C.M. The 80th Battery was another that distinguished itself by exceptional gallantry at Ligny during the retreat, and three of its N.C.Os won the D.C.M. Near the same place the 135th Battery also covered itself with glory. In fact, it is not too much to say that the situation on the afternoon of August 26th was very largely saved by the splendid heroism of our Field Artillery; and for the exploits of this branch of the service alone the battle of Le Cateau must always stand out as a bright spot in the annals of British arms.

The Germans did not pursue the 3rd Division beyond the line of the villages above named. In the case of the 5th Division there was no pursuit at all, in the strict sense of the term. That is to say, there were no rear-guard actions. The division made its way through Reumont, to the continuation of the straight Roman road by which it had reached Le Cateau, and down this road it continued its retreat unmolested. Rain began to fall heavily and numbers of the men, heedless alike of rain or of pursuing Germans, dropped like logs by the roadside and slept.

The extrication of the Le Cateau army from a position which, on paper, was all but hopeless, was undoubtedly a very fine piece of generalship on the part of Sir Horace Smith-Dorrien. The C. in C. in his despatch wrote:

> I say without hesitation that the saving of the left wing of the army under my command, on the morning of August 26th, could never have been accomplished unless a commander of rare and unusual coolness, intrepidity and determination had been present to personally conduct the operation.

CHAPTER 8

The Retreat From Le Cateau

Le Cateau may without shame be accepted as a defeat. There was at no time, even in anticipation, the possibility of victory. It was an affair on altogether different lines to that of Mons. At Mons the British Army had been set a definite task, which it had cheerfully faced, and which it had carried through with credit to itself and with much advantage to its ally. Its ultimate retirement had only been in conformity with the movements of that ally. Everything worked according to book.

But Le Cateau was quite another affair. Here we find half the British force temporarily cut off from the other half by *force majeure*, and turning at bay on a pursuer whom it could no longer escape. There was never any question of victory. The disparity in numbers and in armament left no room for illusions on that score. Searching deep below the surface, we might perhaps find that the main factor in deciding that Briton and German should cross swords at Le Cateau was the primitive impulse—always strong in the Anglo-Saxon breed—to face an ugly crisis and die fighting. In the event the British force faced the foe, and fought, but it did not die—as an army; a result due to consummate generalship on the part of the Army Corps Commander, aided by a strange laxity, or over-caution, as the case may be, on the part of the enemy.

Why the Germans did not pursue with more vigour will never be known till the history of this period comes to be written from the German side. The failure to pursue after Mons is intelligible. While the 2nd A.C. was defending the group of manufacturing towns north of the Valenciennes road, the 1st A.C. on the right was thrown forward in échelon, and formed a standing menace to the left flank of the advancing enemy. A too eager pursuit, in advance of the general line, might well have resulted in the isolation and capture of the German right.

At Le Cateau, however, there was no such risk. Here the German attack had been mainly concentrated against the 5th Division, evidently with the idea of turning the British right flank, and forcing in a wedge between the 1st and 2nd Army Corps. This was in effect done, and all that remained was for the Germans to push their advantage home in order to separate, at any rate, a large percentage of the 2nd A.C. from the main body on its left. This could have been effected without any fear of a flank attack from the 1st A.C, that corps being at the time far too scattered and distant to make any concerted move; and in any case being hopelessly cut off by the Sambre.

Why this programme was not carried through to its consummation can only be guessed at. It may be that the enemy had only imperfect information as to the movements of the 1st A.C.; or it may be that they were deterred by the knowledge that General d'Amade was hurrying up on their right flank from the direction of Arras with the 61st and 62nd Reserve Divisions; or it may be again that the advancing troops had been too roughly handled by the British at bay to allow of pursuit. This last hypothesis is not only the most flattering to British self-esteem, but it is also eminently possible. In any case the fact remains that they did not pursue. Sir Horace, on the other hand, had no idea of letting this supineness on the part of the enemy influence his own policy.

The troops were kept moving. On the afternoon of the 26th, the 5th Division managed to get back as far as Estrées, and the 3rd Division to Vermand and Hargicourt, each arriving at its destination about dark. The weather was very bad, and the majority of the men were crowded into farm-barns, but many dropped by the roadside where they were and slept, heedless of the pouring rain.

On the far side of the river the 4th and 6th Brigades, whom we last saw at Landrecies and Maroilles, got to Etreux and Hannappes respectively about 2 p.m., and bivouacked by the roadside; but the 5th Brigade, moving by way of Taisnières and Prisclies, could get no further than Barzy, and was therefore still far behind the line of the 2nd A.C. retreat, and, in fact, of its own division. The 2nd Brigade got to Oisy without mishap. The 1st Brigade was not so fortunate, the Munster Fusiliers being overtaken at Bergues and captured *en masse* with the exception of some 150 who escaped with the aid of the 15th Hussars. Two guns of the 118th Battery, which were with them were captured at the same time. A mile or two further south, on the high ground just beyond Etreux, the brigade was again attacked, the Black Watch, who were then doing rear-guard, coming under a severe artillery fire. This was most effectively replied to by the 117th Battery under Major Packard and the pursuit was checked. The battery in withdrawing was charged by a squadron of German cavalry, but the charge died away under the fire of the Black Watch.

The story of the rescue of the Munsters by the 15th Hussars is one of which the latter regiment may well be proud. Two troops only of the 15th Hussars were engaged, and yet the number of honours that fell to them is remarkable. Mr. Nicholson got the Cross of the Legion of Honour, Sergeant Papworth got the Victoria Cross, and Sergeant Blishen, Corporal Shepherd and Corporal Aspinall the D.C.M.

The story of this affair is as follows: It was reported to the General commanding that the Munster Fusiliers were in trouble, and the 15th Hussars, who were acting as divisional cavalry, were sent back to help. The country in the neighbourhood of Bergues is a difficult one, being traversed by numerous narrow byways cutting in all directions, and the 15th Hussars, not knowing just where the Munster Fusiliers were, separated into troops and beat the country northwards. Just south of Bergues, where the road from that place meets the main road to La Capelle, Mr. Nicholson's troop found 150 of the Munster Fusiliers in great difficulties, with some Germans in pursuit not 200 yards distant. He at once dismounted the troop and, sending the horses off for shelter to a farmyard behind, lined the hedges on the side of the main road and opened fire on the Germans. These retired to a farm some 200 yards up the road, from which they presently brought a machine-gun to bear on the hedges, and under cover of this they shortly afterwards emerged, driving a herd of cattle before them down the road. The Hussars, however, shot down both cattle and Germans and sent the survivors scuttling back once more into the farm.

In the meanwhile the Hon. E. Hardinge's troop, having heard the firing, arrived on the scene from another direction and—also dismounting—crept up to a position from which they could command the farmyard, and opened fire on the Germans massed inside, doing tremendous execution at first, as it was a complete surprise. The Germans, however, quickly recovered themselves and returned the fire with machine-guns. Almost at the first discharge Mr. Hardinge fell mortally wounded, and Sergeant Papworth took over command of the troop.

Bodies of the enemy were now seen advancing on all sides, and it was obvious that, if the little British force was to escape being surrounded, it was time to move. There is always a disposition on such occasions for very tired men to throw up the sponge and surrender. In the present instance, however, any such inclination was summarily checked by the energy and determination of Mr. Nicholson and Sergeant Papworth, who, taking prompt charge of the situation, brought the whole party—Munsters and all—safely out of the difficulty. They had to put in twenty-eight miles of steady marching before they finally caught up with their division.

On the 27th the retreat was resumed, the troops starting as usual in the small hours of the morning. The 1st Division, in place of following the route taken by the 2nd Division, crossed the Sambre and went through Wassigny to Hauteville; the 2nd Division went to Mont d'Origny, and the 3rd and 5th Divisions joined up at Ham, the former, which had been greatly harassed and delayed throughout by hostile cavalry and horse artillery, arriving some hours after the other. On arrival at its destination the whole division dropped by the side of the road and slept.

Next morning the whole 2nd A.C. followed the one road from Ham to Noyon, the 5th Division, which was still some hours ahead of the 3rd, passing on through Noyon to Pommeraye, where it billeted.

On the other side of the river the two divisions of the 1st A.C. also joined up and went through La Fère to the group of villages to the south of that place, where they billeted, the 1st Brigade at St.

Gobain, the 2nd at Frésancourt, the 4th at Berlancourt, the 5th at Servais and the 6th at Deuillet and Amigny.

The monotony of retreat was in some part relieved by several rear-guard brushes during the day between the 3rd and 5th C.B. on the one hand and some Prussian Uhlans of the Guard on the other, in one and all of which the honours rested very emphatically with the British cavalry.

The 29th August, 1914, will probably be imprinted for ever in the minds of those who took part in the famous Mons retreat, for on this day the troops rested. For eight days they had now been marching practically without ceasing and the feet of many were literally stripped of skin; they had dug trenches innumerable and had fought various engagements, great and small, for the most part in the blazing heat of an exceptionally hot August, and with a minimum of sleep and food. But on the 29th they rested.

The whole expeditionary force was now once more in touch, and, with its arrival at the La Fère line, the acute pressure of the retreat may be said to have been at an end. The various divisions were re-organized; mixed up brigades were once more sorted out; stragglers and "temporarily attached" restored to their lost battalions, and the whole force put into ship-shape working order. General Sordet, who had rendered incalculable service with his cavalry on our left flank, was now relieved by the 6th French army, which came into position on our left in the neighbourhood of Roye, while the 5th French army continued our line towards the east. The British army, in fact, refreshed by its rest on the 29th, was now in perfect trim to turn and fight at any moment. But this was not to be for awhile yet. General Joffre's scheme called for a still further retirement.

At 1 p.m. on the 29th the French Generalissimo visited the C. in C. at his headquarters at Compiègne and explained to him the outline of his plan. Sir Douglas Haig, Sir Horace Smith-Dorrien and General Allenby were also present. As a result of this conference, the bridges over the Oise were blown up (an operation which again cost us some good lives from among the R.E.), and the British force retired another twenty miles to a line north of the Aisne, between Soissons and Compiègne.

The 2nd A.C. set out on this march about 3 p.m.; the 1st A.C.

followed some twelve hours later, marching in one column through the Forêt de St. Gobain, after which it divided up, the 1st Division going to L'Allemande and the 2nd Division to Passy.

On the morning of the 31st the march was once more resumed, the 2nd Division leaving at 6.30 a.m. and marching via Pernaut and Cutry to Soucy, which was reached at 4.30 p.m., while the 1st Division retired to Missy-à-Bois.

The 3rd A.C. took a wrong turn near Vellerie this day and for a time lost themselves, but in the end joined up with the new line, which reached—broadly speaking—from Crépy to Villers-Cotterêts.

CHAPTER 9
Villers-Cotterêts

At the latter place we were again forced into a rear-guard action. At nine o'clock the 4th (Guards') Brigade, which was acting rear-guard, was overtaken at Soucy, where—in accordance with orders—it had faced about while the 2nd Division was having a two hours' halt for rest and dinner. It was no case of surprise, the brigade being thoroughly prepared and, indeed, expecting to have to hold the enemy in check.

Dispositions were therefore made accordingly. The 2nd Grenadiers and 3rd Coldstream held the ground from Montgobert to Soucy, with the Coldstream lining the long grass ride that runs through the woods at Haramont. They were supported by two batteries of the 41st Brigade R.F.A. The 2nd Coldstream and Irish Guards were posted in rear of the first line along the northern edge of the Forêt de Villers-Cotterêts, at the base of the ridge known as the Rond de la Reine.

The enemy commenced by shelling the front line, and shelling it with such accuracy that General Scott-Ker ordered the Grenadiers and 3rd Coldstream to fall back through the 2nd line and take up a position in rear. This was done, but subsequently these two battalions were brought up into line with the Irish Guards along the northern edge of the wood, whilst the 2nd Coldstream were sent back to take up a covering position in rear of the wood, along the railway east and west of Villers-Cotterêts Halte. Such was the position without much change up to midday, when the enemy's attack began to slacken and shortly afterwards they appeared to have had enough of it and drew off. The 4th Brigade thereupon resumed its march as far as Thury, which was reached about 10.30 p.m. Their casualties in this action amounted to over 300. The Irish Guards had Colonel the Hon. G. Morris and Lieutenant Tisdall killed; Major Crichton and Lord Castlerosse wounded. In the Grenadiers the Hon. J. Manners and Lieutenant McDougall were killed, and in the Coldstream, Lieutenant G. Lambton was killed and Captain Burton and Captain Tritton wounded. The Brigadier-General Scott-Ker was himself badly wounded in the thigh, and the command of the brigade was taken over by Colonel Corry.

CHAPTER 10
Néry

The same morning witnessed a very heroic little action at Néry. During the preceding night the 1st C.B. had billeted in this little village, together with L Battery R.H.A., which was attached to the brigade. The village lies low in a broken and hilly country. To the south and east of it the ground rises suddenly and very steeply, forming a long ridge which juts out into the plain from the north. Along these heights Lieutenant Tailby, of the 11th Hussars, was patrolling in the early morning, and in a very thick fog, when he suddenly bumped right into a column of German cavalry. He had hardly time to gallop back and warn the brigade before shot and shell began to fly thickly into the village. The German force, as it afterwards turned out, consisted of no less than six cavalry regiments, with two batteries of six guns each attached; and there is reason to believe that they were just as surprised at the encounter as was the 1st C.B. However that may be, the advantage in position, as well as in numbers, was greatly on the side of the Germans, who, from the heights they were on, completely dominated the ground below. Even the sun favoured them, for when that broke through about five o'clock, it was at the backs of the enemy and full in the faces of the defenders.

The lifting of the fog soon cleared up any doubts in the minds of all concerned as to how matters stood. On the heights above, with the sun behind them, were the six German regiments, dismounted, with their twelve guns. Down below in an open orchard on the western side of the village were the Bays and L Battery R.H.A. They were still in the position in which they had bivouacked the night previous. Beyond them were the 5th Dragoon Guards. The

11th Hussars were on the south-east side of the village nearest the enemy, but more or less hidden from view and protected from the enemy's fire by the lie of the land.

Then began one of those rare episodes which will live for ever in history and romance.

The position of L Battery had not been chosen with a view to action. Except for the fog, it would never have been caught there; but having been caught there it accepted the situation. Owing to the broken nature of the ground, only three of its guns could be brought to bear on the enemy's position, but these three were quickly at work. The Bays, who were the regiment chiefly in the line of fire, got their horses into safety and then joined in with rifle and machine-gun fire, taking what shelter they could; but this did not amount to much, and the sun was in their eyes. None of these disadvantages made themselves felt in the case of the 11th Hussars, who, from their sheltered position, were able to bring a most effective machine-gun fire to bear on the flank of the Germans. Their doings, however, we may pass by. The focus-point of German attention was the little Horse Artillery Battery down in the apple-orchard. This now became the target for a perfect tornado of shot and shell, and at a range of only 400 yards. Two of the three guns were quickly knocked out, and the fire of batteries, rifles and maxims became concentrated on the one that remained.

Men and officers combined to serve this one gun. Captain Bradbury, in command, had one leg taken off by a shell, but he propped himself up, and continued to direct the fire till he fell dead. Lieutenant Campbell died beside him, as did also Brigadier-Major Cawley, who came up with orders from headquarters. Lieutenant Gifford and Lieutenant Mundy both fell wounded, and Sergeant-Major Dorrell took over command. With the support of Sergeant Nelson, Gunner Darbyshire and Driver Osborne he cheerfully continued this absurd and unequal duel.

In the meanwhile the 5th Dragoon Guards had been ordered to work round to the north-east, in order to make a diversion from that flank. This they were able to do to a certain extent, though at some cost, Colonel Ansell being shot through the head and killed at the very outset. The regiment, however, were not strong enough, single-handed, to make more than a demonstration, and the whole situation was far from promising when, by the mercy of Providence, the 4th C.B. most unexpectedly arrived on the scene from the direction of Compiègne. These lost no time in dismounting and joining up with the 5th Dragoon Guards, the four combined regiments pouring a steady fire into the flank of the enemy.

This new development entirely changed the aspect of affairs, and, finding the situation getting rather too hot for them, the Germans made off hurriedly in the direction of Verrines, abandoning eight of their guns and a maxim.

They tried in the first instance to man-handle their guns out of action, but the steady fire of the cavalry on their flank, supplemented now by a frontal fire from the Bays, who had by this time installed their machine-gun in the sugar factory to the west of the village, proved too much for them, and they abandoned the attempt. The whole affair had so far lasted little over an hour; but the last word had yet to be said, for the 11th Hussars jumped on to their horses, galloped off in pursuit and captured fifty horses and a number of prisoners. The German casualties in killed and wounded were also considerable, and on our side the troops in the open orchard suffered very severely. The Bays showed great daring and activity throughout, Mr. de Crespigny particularly distinguishing himself. They lost seven officers, and out of L Battery only three men emerged unwounded. To the survivors of this battery, however, it must for ever be a source of gratification to reflect that the last shot in that preposterous duel was fired by the battered and bloodstained thirteen-pounder down in the apple-orchard, and that it was fired at the backs of the enemy.

Captain Bradbury, Sergeant-Major Dorrell and Sergeant Nelson were awarded the Victoria Cross, the former posthumously. The last two named were also given their commissions. Lieutenant Gifford got the Cross of the Legion of Honour, and the entire battery earned a name which will live as long as history. There is a sequel to this gallant little affair which is sufficiently satisfactory to record. The 1st and 4th C.B. billeted that night at Borest, and continued their progress south next day through the Forêt d'Ermenonville. Here, abandoned among the birch trees of the forest, they found two of the guns which the Germans had succeeded in getting away from Néry. It was a small incident, but very satisfactory as a finale.

CHAPTER 11

The Advance to the Aisne

On the following day, September 2nd, the British force found itself facing the Marne from the north bank, and the whole of September 3rd was occupied in getting the troops across, an operation of some little delicacy, as it involved in many cases the exposure of our flank to the enemy. During the process of transit the whole of the British cavalry—which had hitherto been distributed along the length of our line—was concentrated by the river side in the open ground at Gournay. By nightfall the whole force was on the south side and the bridges had been blown up.

The following day saw the end of the great retreat. There was, it was true, a further retirement of some twelve miles to a line running from Lagny to Courtagon, but this last proved to be the southernmost point of France which our troops were destined to see.

The British army had now in twelve days covered a distance from Mons of 140 miles as the crow flies, and of considerably more as troops march. During these twelve days two pitched battles had been fought, in addition to many rear-guard actions and cavalry skirmishes. The bulk of the fighting had so far fallen on the 2nd A.C., whose casualties already amounted to 350 officers and 9,200 men. However, the long, demoralizing retreat had now at last reached the turning-point. At Rebaix we picked up 2,000 fresh troops belonging to the 6th Division. These had been trained up from the mouth of the Loire, Havre being no longer reckoned safe, and were a welcome stiffening to the footsore veterans from Mons.

The period that follows is familiarly known as the battle of the Marne, a broad classification which—as such—is allowable, but which is apt to mislead. In the strict sense there was no battle during the British advance. The fighting that took place between September 5th and September 14th was desultory, and was chiefly in the nature of independent and—to a great extent—disconnected engagements, mostly of the advance guard and rear-guard type. The tributaries of the Marne, the Grand Morin and the Petit Morin were each defended, the latter as stubbornly as was the Marne itself, and, in point of fact, some of the hardest fighting which the advancing army met with was on the 10th, after the Marne had been left well behind.

The advance at first was slow and cautious. When an army has for fourteen days been systematically falling back before an enemy, the only casualties within its ken are its own. It may be assumed—and with every right—that there are also killed and wounded among the pursuing force. But they are never seen. Only khaki-clad figures fill the field ambulances; only khaki-clad figures are left behind in the hospitals, and in the cemeteries and roadside trenches. The ever-swelling roll of "missing" is all on one side. There are no missing among those who pursue. In such circumstances, to the tired soldier-mind the pursuing enemy becomes in time invested with a species of invulnerability. At the end of fourteen days that enemy has assumed an altogether fictitious value for evil; it becomes a death-dealing engine, relentlessly sweeping up wounded and stragglers, and itself showing no scars; it inspires an all but superstitious dread. To such a frame of mind the sight of a few grey-clad figures stretched upon the ground and a few groups of grey-clad prisoners marching to the rear acts as a very salutary tonic. The scales drop from the eyes; the glamour of the unknown fades away, and the enemy sinks from its apotheosis to the level of mere mortal clay.

It took two days for this new spirit to get hold of the British force feeling its way northward. Then it got confidence and began to push; and in exact ratio to the vigour of its push was the tale of prisoners and guns captured.

The turn of the tide came on September 5th. On that day General Joffre told the C. in C. that he was going to take the offensive. The German advance had—as all the world now knows—swerved off from Paris towards the south-east, thereby half exposing its right flank to the 6th French army. General Joffre quickly made the exposure complete by wheeling that army towards the east, at the same time throwing forward the left of his line. Von Kluck was quick to realize that he was in a tight place, and with characteristic promptitude cleared out northwards. The pursued army spun on its heels and followed, but followed at first with an excess of caution which was perhaps excusable in a tired army to whom anything but retreat was a new experience.

At the moment of the above surprising change in the tide of war, the 6th French Army line ran due north and east from Erme-nonville to Lagny. This line was pressing eastward. The British force lay between Lagny and Courtagon, facing north, and in a continu-ation of the same line on our right came Conneau's cavalry and the 6th French Army.

September 6th, which was practically the first day of the advance, saw little fighting, our troops advancing some ten miles only to the line of the Grand Morin, which was not defended with any great show of vigour. We took a few prisoners only, and some maxims.

On the 7th there was much more doing, but it was chiefly cav-alry work. McCracken's 7th Brigade, however, met with a fairly stubborn resistance at Coulommiers, in the course of which the S. Lancs sustained a good many casualties. De Lisle's 2nd C.B. was, as usual, in the forefront of all that was doing. This brigade got in touch with the enemy soon after leaving Fretoy. The 9th Lancers, who were doing advance guard to the brigade, pushed on, how-ever, with great boldness, till they reached the village of Moncel, which was found to be in occupation of German cavalry. Without a moment's hesitation, and without any knowledge of the strength opposed to it, the leading troop took the village at a gallop and cleared it of the enemy. They were, however, themselves compelled shortly afterwards to withdraw, as two fresh squadrons of the en-emy—who proved to be the 1st Guard Dragoons—came down on the village from the north. At the same time a third squadron appeared to the west of the village. These new arrivals were at once charged by Colonel Campbell and Major Beale-Brown at top speed with a troop and half of the 9th Lancers. They rode clean through the Germans, who faced the charge, and then—wheeling to the right—the Lancers joined up with the troop that had already entered the village.

The Germans now retreated to the north side of the village. In anticipation of this movement a squadron of the 18th Hussars had already been posted dismounted among the corn stooks on that side. These now opened fire on the retiring Germans, some seventy of whom turned and charged the dismounted Hussars in line. The latter with great nerve and steadiness let the Dragoons get within 100 yards of them, and then practically annihilated them with a volley. Only a dozen escaped.

The casualties among the 2nd C.B. were not heavy, but Colonel Campbell, while leading the charge south of the village, was wounded in the arm by a lance. Captain Reynolds at the same time was very badly wounded in the shoulder, and Lieutenant Allfrey, while trying to extract the lance from the wound, was killed.

The general order was now for the British army to advance to the north-east in the direction of Chateau Thierry and so try and reach the Marne. The country round here, however, was very difficult, especially in the thickly-wooded neighbourhood of the Petit Morin, and the advance was at first slow and cautious. The 8th Brigade on reaching the valley of the Petit Morin met with a strong resistance, which gave it some trouble before it managed to cross at Orly, where the enemy had left six machine-guns strongly posted on the opposing slope. However, after J Battery R.H.A.—which had displayed the greatest gallantry throughout these operations—had pounded the position for some time, the 4th Middlesex under Colonel Hull (now the only colonel left in the 8th Brigade) and the R. Scots drew up on the edge of the wood topping the narrow valley, and at a given signal dashed down the slope to the bridge and up the far side; whereupon the Germans made off, abandoning their machine-guns, and the position was won.

In the course of this advance the R. Scots lost 2nd Lieutenant Hewat, who was killed, and Lieutenant Hay, who was badly wounded by two bullets in the side, but the casualties among the rank and file were not heavy. They captured some 200 prisoners in the village of Orly. The 2nd Division at La Trétoire met with a very similar resistance, but here the 2nd and 3rd Coldstream and some of the cavalry managed to get across higher up at La Force, and turned the flank of the resistance. The enemy's defence—as at Orly—proved to emanate from few men but many mobile machine-guns, which, by the time the passage had been forced, were far beyond pursuit or capture, but which had been as effective for purposes of obstruction as a brigade. The Coldstream did not dislodge the enemy without casualties, among those wounded being the Hon. C. Monk, Lieutenant Trotter, Sir R. Corbet and 2nd Lieutenant Jackson.

On the same day on the right of the line the Black Watch and the Camerons, the latter of whom had now been appointed to the 1st Brigade vice the Munster Fusiliers, did some very fine work between Bellot and Sablonière, and took a quantity of prisoners; but they had to fight hard for them, and both regiments had a number of casualties, Captain Dalgleish and the Hon. M. Drummond in the Black Watch being killed. The 1st C.B. co-operated with the two Scotch regiments by attacking the village of Sablonière, which was finally captured, together with many prisoners, by the 11th Hussars. In addition to this little cavalry success, the 3rd and 5th C.B. each had an encounter this day with German cavalry, and in both instances maintained the unquestioned superiority of the British in this particular arm of the service.

At five o'clock on the morning of the 9th the 2nd A.C. started out for the Marne. The whole A.C. had to cross by the one bridge at Chailly, so the operation was a protracted one, but by dark they were all across and had pushed ahead some miles north of the river. A German battery on the heights above Nanteint was attacked with great determination and captured by the Lincolns during this advance, the Germans sticking with great gallantry to their guns till every man of the battery had been killed or wounded.

The 3rd A.C, on the left of the 2nd, had considerable trouble in crossing at La Ferté. Here the bridge had been destroyed, and the north bank was strongly held by the enemy (with machine-guns as usual). The R.E. came to the rescue with a pontoon bridge, but the German fire was persistent, and it was night before the bridge was completed.

The 1st A.C. in the meanwhile had crossed at Chateau Thierry, but not without some destructive opposition from machine-guns.

On the morning of the 10th the advance became a race between the 5th and the 2nd Divisions. These two set out northwards at 5 a.m. covered by Gough with the 3rd and 5th C.B. The 3rd Division had been stopped at Germigny, and had consequently fallen behind, and the 4th and 6th Divisions—as we have seen—had to put up with a long wait at La Ferté. The advance was therefore in the shape of a wedge, the effect of which was to threaten the flank of the Germans in front of the 6th French Army and cause them to retire with considerable haste. By midday, however, the 3rd Division on our left had all but come up into line, and the formation became more orthodox again. Our aeroplanes, favoured by beautiful weather, were now doing fine work, and, by the information they gave, made it possible to push the advance right up to the line of the Ourcq. There was little serious opposition, but desultory fighting took place here and there all along the line, and at Montreuil the Cornwalls suffered some serious losses.

We captured a number of prisoners during this advance to the Ourcq. The 9th Brigade alone took 600 north of Germigny, and at Haute Vesnes the 6th Brigade captured 400 and put as many more *hors de combat*, the 1st K.R.R., who were well supported by the 50th Battery R.F.A., being the main contributors to this result. In all, we took over 2,000 prisoners that day and many guns. The woods were everywhere full of stragglers, many of whom were only too glad to surrender. Others, however, put up a fight and were only taken after a stubborn resistance.

On the 11th General Joffre shifted the advance half a point to the east, the effect of which was to narrow the front of the British troops and so cause a good deal of congestion on the few roads at our disposal.

On this day a sudden and very abominable change came over the weather, the wind chopping round to the north-west, and the temperature dropping in one day from great heat to bitter cold. Rain fell continuously, and there was wide-spread lamentation over the greatcoats thrown away in the heat of the Mons retreat.

CHAPTER 12

The Passage of the Aisne

On September 12th the battle of the Aisne may be said to have begun. The first and second stages of the war, the retreat from Mons, and the advance from the Grand Morin, were of the past. The third stage—the passage and occupation of the Aisne by our troops— covers a period of some four weeks, the greater part of which was, comparatively speaking, barren of incident. The first three days, how- ever, were eventful, and the 14th saw one of the most stubbornly contested battles of the war. This will be dealt with in its place.

The 12th saw the first real check to our fifty-mile advance. Very early in the day it became apparent to our commanders that the retreat of the Germans had been in accordance with a plan pre- arranged (in the event of certain happenings) and that the pursued now definitely stood at bay. The situation was not one to encour- age a reckless offensive. A wide valley some two miles across, down the centre of which wound the sluggish Aisne, now swollen and discoloured by the rains; steep down-like bluffs on either side of the valley, furrowed by deep-cut roads that twisted down to the lower ground—the bluffs in many places thickly and picturesquely wooded. To the west Soissons, to the east Rheims; and in face, on the opposite slope, the great German army. It was not known at the time that, on the Craonne plateau crowning the slopes op- posite, the forethought of the Germans had prepared in advance a complete system of very elaborate trenches, of a kind then new to warfare, but since horribly familiar. These were supplemented in many cases by the old stone quarries and caves which run the length of the heights.

Such was the scene in which the German and the Allied armies were destined to face one another for over a year, dealing out ceaseless death, desolation and pain, and gaining no fraction of military advantage for either side. That this was so is now history, but on September 12th, 1914, the future was still the future, and neither side had as yet had experience of the dead-wall method of fighting which has ever since characterized the Great War. The British commanders therefore, and the troops under them, prepared to push on with all the enthusiasm inspired by the events of the past week.

The first honours in the opening of this new act of the war-drama fell to the 1st C.B. who in the early hours of the morning were ordered to get possession of the village of Braine, a place of some importance, as it commanded the only road down to Missy on the southern side of the valley. The place was held by a battalion of German infantry, the houses loop-holed, and the streets barricaded. The 1st C.B. advanced from Cerseuil to the edge of the valley, and, leaving their horses on the high ground, made down the slope to the river on foot. The place was stubbornly defended, and was not taken without a certain amount of loss on our side, Captain Springfield in the Bays being killed, and Captain Pinching wounded, but after some rather fierce house-to-house fighting in the main street, the place was eventually captured and cleared of the enemy by nine o'clock, the German casualties amounting to some 300.

Sir Hubert Hamilton thereupon advanced the 3rd Division to Brenelle, while Sir Charles Fergusson passed on with the 5th Division through the captured village of Braine to Sermoise. Away on the right the 1st and 2nd Divisions advanced as far as Courcelles and Vauxcéré.

The first infantry division to come into action in the Aisne valley was the 4th, under General Snow, who—having crossed the Ourcq unopposed—arrived at Buzancy on the morning of the 12th and found the right of the 6th French Army bombarding the Germans, who were in occupation of the Mont de Paris, just south of Soissons. Snow at once chimed in with his own guns, and a tremendous artillery duel resulted, in which the Germans after a time threw up the sponge and made off across the Soissons bridge, which they destroyed behind them.

Map showing line occupied by British
troops after the battle of the Aisne.

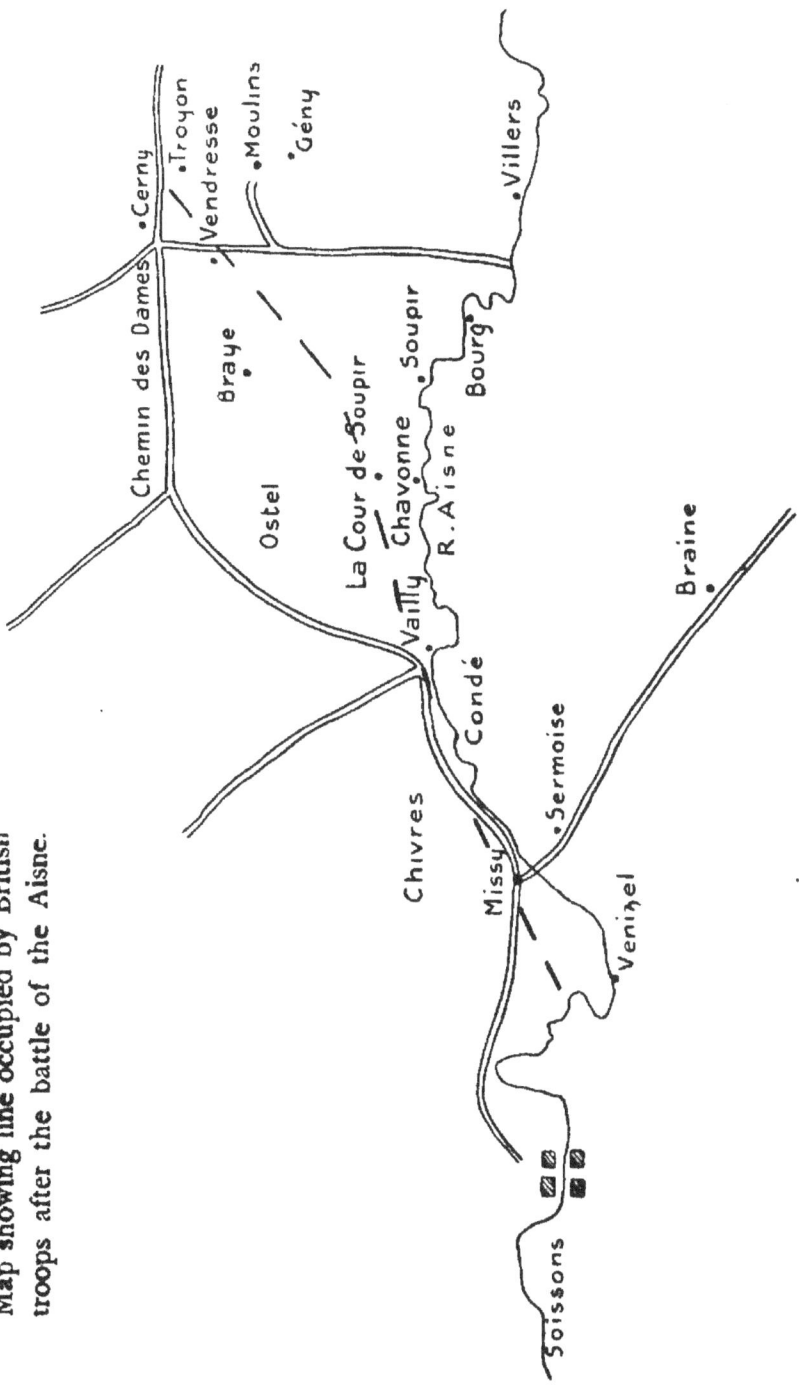

Cerny

Troyon

Vendresse

Moulins

Géry

Chemin des Dames

Braye

Villers

Ostel

La Cour de Soupir

Chavonne

Soupir

Vailly

R. Aisne

Bourg

Condé

Chivres

Braine

Sermoise

Missy

Venizel

Soissons

The 3rd and 5th C.B. were in the meantime at Chaudun awaiting developments.

The south side of the Aisne was now clear of the enemy, and the problem arose as to how best to get our troops across. The weather was still as bad as could be, with a bitter cold driving rain from the north-west which made any air reconnaissance an impossibility. It was essential, however, to learn the state of the bridges, so other means had to be devised. The Missy bridge was of especial importance, and Lieutenant Pennycuik, R.E., volunteered to find out all about this by floating down the river on an improvised raft. This he succeeded in doing, at no little risk to himself, and reported the bridge practically destroyed, the north end having been blown up. The bridge at Condé was intact but inaccessible, the long, straight approach to it being open to concentrated machine-gun fire throughout. It had obviously been left as a bait, and to have attempted it would have been to have played straight into the enemy's hands. The question was, in fact, discussed between the C. in C. and Sir Horace, but they decided that, as its capture could only be effected at a great sacrifice of life, and as its possession was strategically of very little value to the enemy, it should be left alone.

On our extreme right near Bourg there was no trouble about crossing, the aqueduct, which here carries the canal across the river, having survived the attempts of the enemy to blow it up; and by this the 1st Division and some of the cavalry and artillery crossed easily enough during the middle of the day on the 13th, and pushed forward some three or four miles along the Laon road. The rest of the cavalry crossed further up the river at Villers. This wing of the army met with very little systematic opposition, but desultory shell-fire and machine-gun fire was going on all the time, and the 1st Scots Guards had some casualties, Houldsworth being killed and Monckton and Balfour wounded.

By nightfall the 1st Brigade had reached Moulins, the 2nd and 3rd Brigades being at Gény. The 5th Brigade had succeeded in reaching Pont d'Arcy by 9 a.m., but found the bridge there destroyed, one solitary girder partly submerged alone remaining, and by this they scrambled across in single file, with a blind shell-fire playing all around. Single girders, however, are not recognized as a military means of communication, so the R.E. set to work to build a pontoon bridge alongside.

The 4th Brigade, on the left of the 2nd Division, had the worst time this day; they made an attempt to cross at Chavonne itself, but were vigorously opposed, the enemy being in possession of the village, and keeping up a ceaseless machine-gun fire which cost us some good men. The Irish Guards were the chief sufferers, especially in officers, Captain Berners, Lord Guernsey and Lord Arthur Hay being killed. However, late in the afternoon, some of the 2nd Coldstream got themselves ferried across in a small boat which was found—minus oars—higher up the river, whereupon the enemy, who as usual were weak in numbers, but strong in machine-guns, made off. The rest of the brigade then crossed in single file by the remains of the bridge, which—like that at Pont d'Arcy—still offered a shaky foothold from shore to shore.

CHAPTER 13

Troyon

The 14th of September probably saw more real fighting in the old-fashioned sense than any other day in which the British troops had been engaged. The whole line covering a frontage of twenty miles was involved, but the fiercest conflict was always on the right with the 1st A.C. This day's fighting is sometimes referred to as the battle of the Aisne, and sometimes as the battle of Troyon. The former is too indefinite, in view of the protracted fighting on the river of that name; the latter is too parochial. In real truth there were four distinct but synchronous battles taking place that day along our front, *viz.*, at Troyon, Verneuil, Soupir and Chivres. The most sanguinary, and undoubtedly the most important as far as results go, was the first of these. It may fairly be said that the British victory at Troyon on September 14th was one of the most brilliant achievements of the war. The generalship displayed was of a high order, and the troops engaged behaved with the greatest steadiness and courage.

Proceedings commenced at the very first streak of dawn. General Bulfin's 2nd Brigade, which had got as far as Moulins on the 13th, set out at four o'clock on the following morning along the road to Vendresse. This road runs between the wooded downs on either side, and the idea was to bring the rest of the 1st Division along it as soon as the heights to right and left had been cleared. Half a mile short of Vendresse the R. Sussex, the 60th and the Northamptons scaled the downs to the right of the road, and deployed in the order named, the Sussex on the left, the 60th in the middle, and the Northamptons on the right, just east of Troyon.

Beyond the Northamptons were the 1st Coldstream, who had been detached from the 1st Brigade. The Loyal N. Lancashire Regiment remained in reserve down at Vendresse, and about six o'clock the other three battalions of the 1st Brigade came marching through them, along the road towards Cerny. About half a mile further on, these three battalions scaled the heights on the left of the road, so as to continue the line of the 2nd Brigade, which was on the right of the road. Here they deployed and remained till the 3rd Brigade came up on their left some three hours later.

The day was a particularly unpleasant one. There was a cold and persistent rain from the north-west right in the faces of the British, and accompanied by a kind of fog which made it impossible to see clearly for more than a couple of hundred yards ahead, and which was responsible for a good deal of unfortunate confusion through the day as to the identity of friend and foe. It also, as may be supposed, greatly increased the difficulty of our Gunners, who found it impossible to locate the enemy accurately, or to get exact information as to the correctness of their range.

Having dealt with the disposition of the three brigades of the 1st Division, we can now turn to the actual fight at Troyon. The main objective of our attack here was the sugar factory which stands near the five cross-roads on the Chemin des Dames. The factory itself was very strongly held with machine-guns, and was flanked by two batteries of artillery. For a quarter of a mile on each side of it were the German trenches, on the one side running along the Chivy road, and on the other along the Chemin des Dames, the two forming an obtuse angle with the apex at the factory itself. In addition, the enemy had four big eleven-inch guns behind their line, the fire from which greatly harassed our troops all through these operations as they completely outranged our batteries. The approach to this position was over turnip and beet fields, very wet and sticky with clay, and sloping gently upwards towards the factory. As long as the 2nd Brigade was on the steep sides of the downs it was comparatively sheltered from the enemy's fire, but the moment this sloping plateau was reached, a tremendous fire burst upon it at close range from rifles, machine-guns, and from two batteries of artillery, which were in position behind the trenches along the Chemin des Dames.

It is difficult to conceive of conditions more unfavourable for attack: a driving rain in the faces of the assailants, an entrenched enemy, and an uphill approach across clay fields saturated with wet and two feet deep in beet plants. However, the order was to advance, so undeterred by the gaps ploughed in their ranks, the brigade pressed steadily on. The objective of the R. Sussex on the left was the enemy's trenches along the Chivy road. Towards this they pushed on at the slow plodding tramp which was the best pace which could be raised in the circumstances, till they reached the comparative shelter of a sunken lane. In this lane the R. Sussex machine-gun section was able to get a position from which it could partially enfilade the Chivy road trenches, and so effective was its fire from this angle, that after a time a white flag was raised, and several hundred Germans were seen running forward with their hands up. Colonel Montresor and many other officers and men of the Sussex left the lane to accept this surrender, whereupon the enemy, from the factory itself and from the trenches to right and left of it, poured a deadly fire into the confused mass of Germans and British, mowing them down in scores. In this indiscriminate massacre the R. Sussex lost very heavily, Colonel Montresor, Maj. Cookson, and Lieutenants Daun and Hughes being killed, and Captain Cameron wounded. The Germans too suffered severely, but about 200 of them were got safely into the lane and sent off to the rear with a platoon as escort.

The R. Sussex being now very considerably reduced in numbers, the Loyal N. Lancashires were brought up from reserve, one company being sent to support the Sussex, while two and a half companies came up on the right of the 60th, *i.e.*, between the 60th and the Northamptons. These two and a half companies being fresh troops were now ordered to attack the sugar factory. The position of the factory and the lie of the ground has already been described. The Loyal N. Lancashires, in order to carry out the attack as ordered, had to advance over a quarter of a mile of open ground under fire, not only from their front, but from both flanks as well, on account of the angle formed by the German trenches to right and left of the factory. Their casualties during this advance were terrible. The C.O., Maj. Lloyd, and his Adjutant, Captain Howard-Vyse, were killed in the first rush. Fifty per cent of the men fell in crossing that fire-swept zone, but the remainder carried steadily on and, at the point of the bayonet, drove out the enemy and captured the factory, an achievement which must undoubtedly rank as one of the finest of the war.

The R. Sussex now pushed forward again, and Lieutenant Dashwood, the machine-gun officer, got his maxims into the factory, and from there enfiladed the two German batteries along the Chemin des Dames. At the same time some of the R. Sussex and the 60th crept up along the road leading from Vendresse to the factory, till they were in a position to enfilade the German trenches to the east of it. This manoeuvre produced an immediate surrender, the Germans leaving their trenches and hoisting the white flag. Warned, however, by their experience earlier in the day, the British remained prudently under cover of the road, and it was as well they did, for the two German batteries in rear of the trenches at once began bombarding this new situation at point-blank range, with the result that, while the British in the road took no harm, the unfortunate Germans who had tried to surrender were practically wiped out by their own people.

This patriotic act was destined to be the last that these particular batteries performed, for Lieutenant Dashwood with the Sussex machine-guns got on to them from the factory and rendered them incapable of further damage. The horses were all killed, and such gunners as survived made off, abandoning the guns.

The factory itself was not held, being of no military value and presenting a first-class target for the German artillery. Lieutenant Dashwood withdrew his machine-guns to a farm-house some 200 yards down the road, and from this point was able to do considerable execution on the retreating enemy. He was soon, however, located, and Lieutenant Pelham, who was assisting him, was killed. The section, however, ultimately managed to get away safely and rejoin its battalion. The vacated factory was at once heavily bombarded by the enemy, and our troops derived no little satisfaction from seeing shell after shell drop where they were not.

The victory of Troyon was now complete, and it was one of which the troops engaged had every reason to be proud. The results, too, were very far-reaching, the position thus gained being never afterwards wrested from the British troops during their stay at the Aisne.

The casualty list in this sanguinary little fight was a heavy one. The Loyal N. Lancashires lost 15 officers, including their C.O. and Adjutant, and over 500 rank and file. The value of their gallant performance was, however, officially recognized, and Captain Spread, who displayed great courage throughout the day, received the Military Cross. The R. Sussex lost 250 rank and file and 9 officers, also including their colonel, while in the 60th, Major Foljambe, Captain Cathcart, Lieutenant Bond and 2nd Lieutenants Forster, Thompson and Davison were killed.

Whilst the 2nd Brigade plus the 1st Coldstream had been engaged with the factory and the German entrenchments along the Chemin des Dames side of it, the Black Watch and Camerons were busy dislodging the other German wing from their trenches along the Chivy road. This again was a costly affair. The Camerons were enfiladed at close range by the German artillery on the other side of the factory, and had lanes torn through their ranks. Colonel Grant-Duff was killed while heading a bayonet charge of the Black Watch, side by side with his Adjutant, Captain Rowan Hamilton. The 1st Scots Guards, who were on the hill between Vendresse and Troyon, also lost their C.O. as well as their second in command, Colonel Lowther being wounded and Major Garnier killed, as were also Lieutenants Inigo Jones and Thornhill. Sir V. Mackenzie and Lieutenant Stirling-Stuart were wounded at the same time. The Scotsmen, however, did not mean stopping that day, and in spite of desperate losses the Chivy road trenches were finally carried at the point of the bayonet and a number of prisoners taken. But it cost the 1st Brigade 49 officers and 1,100 rank and file.

Much of the success during this day was due to the gallant behaviour of the 116th Battery R.F.A. attached to the 1st Brigade. At an early period in the day this battery, for fear of misdirection in the mist, had worked its guns up into a dangerously exposed position close to the firing line. From here they were able to work great damage to the German defences, but, as a natural consequence, themselves suffered severely in the process. Major

Nicholson, in command of the battery, had been wounded early in the morning while reconnoitring for this position, the command then devolving upon Captain Oliver, who took the battery into action. Some 1,200 rounds were fired during the day, and replenishment of ammunition had to be done entirely by hand, all spare men and drivers being led up in relays by Lieutenant Gardiner. The battery remained exposed to a very galling fire till after nightfall, when it was withdrawn by order of Colonel Geddes, commanding the 25th Brigade R.F.A., as its position was in front of the infantry line actually occupied. Lieutenant Simson, well known as a Rugby International, was killed during the operation. Great courage and devotion to duty was shown by Bombardier Collins, the battery telephonist, who, though painfully wounded early in the proceedings, continued at his post throughout the day. The battery was warmly thanked and praised by General Maxse, commanding the 1st Brigade, for the assistance it had given him.

By noon the 1st and 2nd Brigades were extended in a straight line running east and west through the factory. Eventually, however, the line which was actually occupied and entrenched and maintained throughout the Aisne period against incessant counterattacks had its right resting on the Chemin des Dames half a mile east of the factory, and from there inclined gradually backwards till it reached the river east of Soissons. When we consider that the position won this day on the Chemin des Dames was four miles north of the river, the oblique line thereafter held by the British troops was a lasting monument to the remarkable achievement of the 1st Division on September 14th.

There can be no shadow of doubt that the Germans were completely taken by surprise by the unexpected rapidity of the 1st Division's advance. It was a fine piece of generalship, and had Sir Douglas Haig only had fresh troops to bring up from reserve, it is probable that the Germans would have been swept back another mile or two.

Fresh reserve troops, however, were too great a luxury for our small force. The Loyal N. Lancashires had in the morning been the reserve battalion to the 2nd Brigade, and of these fifty per cent. had fallen. Some of the R. Sussex and 1st Coldstream, as a matter of fact, did penetrate as far as Cerny, following the road from Troyon which cuts through the high ground beyond in a narrow defile. This road was literally choked with the enemy's dead. At Cerny they found every symptom of confusion and surprise, abandoned kits, baggage and munitions, and no sign of organized resistance. The detachment, however, was small, and as it was unsupported on either flank it was deemed wise to retire.

CHAPTER 14
Verneuil

We can now move across on to the next range of heights to the left, and see how it there fared with the 3rd and 5th Brigades. Here matters were neither so eventful nor so decisive as on the Troyon ridge. It was ten o'clock before the 3rd Brigade came up into line, and was ordered to extend to the left and join up with the right of the 2nd Division, which was in the neighbourhood of Braye. While carrying out this order and when within a mile or so of Verneuil, they suddenly came up against two strong German columns which were advancing with some unknown object. The rest of the day's proceedings in this quarter may be briefly described as a series of attacks and counter-attacks, which lasted all through the day, between these two German columns and our 3rd, 5th and 6th Brigades. In the fiercely contested combat between these two forces honours were during the earlier part of the day fairly easy, but towards dusk the Germans sensibly weakened, both in attack and defence, and the British troops undoubtedly had the last word.

The most conspicuous episode in this section of the fighting was a really great performance on the part of an Edinburgh man named Wilson, in the Highland Light Infantry. That battalion had just made a most successful and dramatic charge, led by Sir Archibald Gibson-Craig and Lieutenant Powell (both killed), and had established itself in a forward position with its left on a small wood. From this wood a German machine-gun began playing on the ranks of the battalion with such disastrous accuracy that it soon became clear that either the machine-gun must be silenced or the position evacuated. Private Wilson thought the former alternative preferable, and, getting a K.R.R. man to go with him, crept out towards the wood. The K.R.R. man was shot almost at once, but, quite undeterred, Wilson went on alone, killed the German officer and six men, and single-handed captured the machine-gun and two and a half cases of ammunition. It need scarcely be said that he got the Victoria Cross.

Another Victoria Cross earned this day by another Scotsman was little less remarkable, though of an entirely different order.

Private Tollerton, a fine, powerful man in the Scottish Rifles, noticed an officer fall badly wounded in the firing line. Though himself wounded both in the head and hand, Tollerton carried the officer to a place of safety, after which he himself returned to the firing line and there remained fighting, in spite of his wounds, throughout the day. At dusk he returned to the wounded officer. In the meanwhile the firing line had fallen back, with the result that Tollerton and the officer were left behind. The latter was quite incapable of moving, and Tollerton remained with him for three days and nights, till eventually both were rescued.

CHAPTER 15

Soupir

Once more it is necessary to shift our scene still more to the left and nearer again to the Aisne, where the Cour de Soupir farm stands on the crest of the river bluff.

The capture of this position was the work of the Guards' Brigade. At 8 a.m., at the time when the 1st and 2nd Brigades were in the very thick of their fight at Troyon, the 2nd Division, which was still on the south side of the river, began to cross by the new pontoon bridge at Pont d'Arcy, the 6th Brigade moving up the valley to Braye, while the 5th Brigade fought its way up the wooded slopes above Soupir. These last two brigades, as we have seen, linked up with the 3rd Brigade in the neighbourhood of Verneuil.

The 4th Brigade went down the right bank of the river as far as Chavonne, where it remained till midday, when it got the order to scale the heights in support of the 5th Brigade, which was reported in difficulties. Accordingly the 3rd Coldstream and Irish Guards forced their way up through the woods north of Soupir, while the 2nd Grenadiers and two companies of the 2nd Coldstream made for the hamlet of Les Grouins on the left, where the idea was that they were to get in touch with the 1st Cavalry Division, which was also reported in difficulties. The other two companies 2nd Coldstream stayed in reserve, in a wood clearing on the bluff, half a mile south of La Cour de Soupir farm.

The track from Chavonne to the farm zigzags steeply up the bluff above the river through thick woods. Up this track, now ankle-deep in mud, the Guards scrambled in column of fours till they reached the flatter ground above, where they at once came under very heavy fire from the neighbourhood of the farm. Colonel Feilding, who was acting Brigadier, thereupon deployed the two battalions to the left, and, as soon as the Grenadiers had come up into line on their left flank, the three battalions charged through the mist and rain in the direction of La Cour de Soupir farm. As had been the case with the 2nd Brigade, they were met by a very severe machine-gun and rifle fire at close range, the moment they emerged on to the flatter ground above, and their casualties were very considerable; but, notwithstanding, they kept going, captured the farm and trenches and drove out the enemy with heavy loss.

An unfortunate incident, very similar in many respects to that which had befallen the R. Sussex at Troyon, occurred during the capture of these trenches, and was responsible for the deaths of many good men.

Just to the left of the farm a number of Germans were seen advancing with hands up and white flags. Some of the 3rd Coldstream went out to accept the surrender, whereupon a second line of Germans sprang up, and, firing on friend and foe alike, mowed them down indiscriminately.

There can be little doubt that both this and the Troyon incident on the same day were not acts of deliberate treachery on the part of the Germans, but were purely "no surrender" demonstrations, and were probably aimed more at their compatriots than at the British.

In this engagement the 3rd Coldstream lost Captain Banbury, Lieutenant Ives, Lieutenant Bingham, Lieutenant P. Wyndham, Captain Vaughan and Lieutenant Fane, of whom the first four were killed, and 160 rank and file. The position gained, however, was never afterwards lost, but, from September 14th on, was held by the Guards' Brigade for twenty-nine consecutive days, in the face of a rapid succession of counter-attacks of the fiercest description, this position being singled out by the Germans for their most determined efforts at recapture.

CHAPTER 16

The Aisne

The meteoric advance of the 1st A.C. on the 14th had left the western wing of the British force far behind. Had the 2nd A.C. had the luck to find a bridge which had defied destruction—as was the case at Bourg—there is no knowing but that they might have pushed forward shoulder to shoulder with the 1st A.C. and established themselves on the heights beyond. No such good fortune, however, was theirs. At Venizel, Missy and Vailly the bridges had been successfully demolished and the approaches to the river were everywhere difficult, especially at Missy, where for three-quarters of a mile the ground on the south side of the river lies flat and exposed. The bridge at Condé, as has already been explained, was intact—had, in fact, been designedly left so by the enemy—and for that very reason was outside of consideration as far as the problem of crossing the river was concerned. It became, therefore, a matter for the R.E., and with characteristic prompti-tude that indefatigable corps started in on its work of repair and construction. The work had to be carried out under no small dif-ficulties, and to the accompaniment of a systematic shelling, the enemy on the heights beyond having the exact range of the river. There were considerable casualties among the Engineers. By mid-day, however, on the 14th the work was practically completed, the road bridges at Venizel, Missy and Vailly, and the railway bridge east of Venizel, having been repaired, in addition to which eight pontoon bridges had been thrown over the river at varying in-tervals. This was good work on the part of the R.E., nor did their labours begin and end with the work of repair and construction.

Captain Johnstone[1] and Lieutenant Flint worked below Missy all through this day up to seven o'clock in the evening, bringing back the wounded on rafts and returning with ammunition—all the time under fire. The former got the Victoria Cross for this; the latter the D.S.O.

Handicapped though they were in comparison with the 1st A.C. by the lack of a negotiable bridge, the three divisions at the Soissons end of the line were by no means disposed to sit still while the Sappers were working at their pontoon. The 11th Brigade (in the 4th Division) got itself ferried across below Venizel early in the day, and lost no time in getting into its position to the west of Bucy, where it dug itself in near St. Marguerite. At midday the 12th Brigade were able to cross by the repaired road bridge at Venizel and they at once linked up with the 11th Brigade at Bucy, just in time to take part in an attack which was made upon the Vregny heights opposite at 2 p.m. Meanwhile a pontoon bridge was being built close to the Venizel road bridge, and by 5.30 this, too, was finished, and the 10th Brigade crossed and completed the concentration of the 4th Division.

A mile higher up, at Missy, the 5th Division was in the meantime experiencing great difficulty in getting to the river, the flat ground approaching it being swept by a murderous fire from the far side. The 13th Brigade, in fact, was foiled in all its attempts in this direction, and remained throughout the day at Sermoise. The 14th Brigade, however, managed to cross early in the afternoon at Moulins des Roches and with all the speed possible linked up with the 4th Division on its left, arriving at its post just in time to help in repelling a strong German counter-attack, which was launched against our lines at three o'clock. These two brigades in retaliation made repeated attacks on the Chivres heights during the afternoon, but without success, and at night they fell back to St. Marguerite.

The 3rd Division reached the river at Vailly. Here the bridge had been blown up, but a single plank bridged the gap made at the north end, and by this the 8th and 9th Brigades got across in single file. The 7th Brigade in the meanwhile was getting across on rafts—three men at a time—a slow and tiresome business, which occupied the whole day. It was midday by the time the 9th

1. Killed June 6th, 1915.

Brigade, which followed the 8th, had crossed by the single plank above-mentioned, but they pushed forward at once and secured the heights opposite, the R. Fusiliers establishing themselves well forward on the Maison Rouge spur to the left, and the Lincolns on the Ostel spur, within half a mile of La Cour de Soupir farm held by the Guards. Here they remained all night, but at seven o'clock next morning the R. Fusiliers were heavily attacked and driven back to the Maison Rouge farm, with the loss from among their officers of Captain Byng, Captain Cole, Captain Attwood and 2nd Lieutenant Hobbs. The Northumberland Fusiliers, who had pushed forward along the road up the wooded valley between the spurs, also had serious casualties, and had to withdraw. The Lincolns at the same time were driven from the Ostel spur and by 1 p.m. had re-crossed the river to the south side.

Once more, after another very wet night, the 5th Division on the 15th attacked the Chivres heights, and, once more failing, had to fall back to a line from St. Marguerite to the bank of the river between Sermoise and Condé. There they dug themselves in and there they remained till the end of the Aisne battle. The position was very bad from a strategic point of view, as it was on the low ground by the river, with the Germans only 400 yards away on the heights beyond; but it was the best that could be done. The 5th Division was greatly upset at its second failure to take the Chivres heights. It did not realize (as, indeed, who did at that time?) that the Allied advance had reached its farthest north, and that the Chivres heights were to remain untaken by either French or English for very many months to come.

The failure of the British left to advance encouraged the Germans to deliver counter-attacks all along the line, especially against the advanced position held by the 1st A.C. These, however, failed just as completely as had our own attempt to advance on the left. Several very determined attacks were made against the Guards' Brigade at the Soupir farm, but all were repulsed with heavy loss.

The enemy was all this time steadily outranging our artillery with its big eleven-inch guns, popularly known as "Black Marias." The difficulty of properly entrenching against this long-range cannonade was greatly increased by the scarcity of proper tools, but, by means of a mixed assortment of implements, borrowed from the farms, a certain amount of protection was secured, and this was steadily improved upon from day to day. It began to be realized by now, by all parties concerned, that these entrenchments were likely to be rather more permanent than the emergency ditches scooped out with hands and mess-tins at Mons and Le Cateau, and in point of fact the line held at this time remained practically unchanged till the removal of the troops to Flanders.

On the right the 1st A.C. held the ground from the Chemin des Dames through Chivy to La Cour de Soupir. On their left was the 3rd Division about a mile to the north of Vailly. Then came the gap caused by the bridge at Condé being in the German hands. Beyond this the 5th Division—as we have seen—held the ground from the bend in the river east of Missy to St. Marguerite; and beyond St. Marguerite the 4th Division joined up with the 6th French Army. The 6th Division arrived at this time, thus technically completing General Pulteney's 3rd A.C. As a matter of fact, however, the C. in C., at the first, utilized the greater part of this division to strengthen the 1st A.C. on the right, where the greatest German pressure was being felt, the remainder being held in reserve.

About noon on the 16th, the line held by the Guards' Brigade at the Soupir farm, always the special object of German attention, was treated to an exceptionally violent bombardment. So accurate, in fact, was this fire, that the Brigadier-General ordered a temporary retirement to the shelter of the road behind and below. Very shortly after this retirement had taken place, it was seen that a barn at one end of the farm buildings, which had just been vacated, was on fire. This barn was being used as a temporary hospital, and in it at the time were some fifty wounded Germans. It was clearly a case for very prompt action and very risky action, but there was no hesitation about it. Without the loss of a moment, Major Matheson, who at the time was commanding the 3rd Coldstream, called for volunteers, and accompanied by Major Steele and Drs. Huggan and Shields and some men of No. I Company under Lord Feilding, he rushed forward through the shell-fire to the blazing building. All concerned worked with such goodwill that every wounded man was successfully got into safety and with few casualties on our side, but a few minutes later Dr. Huggan, who had been very active in the rescue work, was killed by a shell which burst in a quarry into which some of the wounded had been carried. The same shell killed twelve others, including three officers of the 52nd Oxford Light Infantry who were attached at the time to the Guards' Brigade, and wounded fifty more. Dr. Huggan, who was best known as a Scotch International football player, had greatly distinguished himself on former occasions, both at Landrecies and Villers-Cotterêts, by his courage and devotion to the wounded. He was buried in the garden of the farm.

The 16th was otherwise an uneventful day, but on the 17th there was a good deal of fighting here and there, enlivened by some fine individual acts of bravery and devotion.

An incident on the right of our line at this time attracted much attention on account of the German methods which it disclosed—methods with which we afterwards became much more familiar. At the village of Troyon a captain and two subalterns and 160 men of the Northamptons had entrenched themselves by the roadside some distance ahead of the main body. Two hundred and fifty yards to their front, and separated from them by a turnip field, was a German entrenchment containing from 400 to 500 men. For five days the Northants men had to remain in trenches which were knee deep in water. Rain fell ceaselessly, and on the 17th seemed to come down harder than ever. Ague appeared among the men, and considerably reduced their effective strength. On the 15th the captain in command showed himself for a moment above the trench and was at once killed. Shortly afterwards the senior lieutenant was also killed. The command then devolved upon the junior lieutenant, who had less than a year's service.

On the 17th—to the surprise of all—the Germans were seen advancing across the turnip field holding up their hands. It was to be assumed that they too had had enough of their water-logged trenches. The Northamptons, naturally gratified at this surrender, left the trench to meet them. When, however, the German officer saw how few men they had to deal with, he changed his mind and ordered his men to charge. The young lieutenant promptly shot the German officer and a sergeant with his revolver, but was himself immediately shot down, though, strange to say, not killed. The affair, however, would obviously have gone very badly for the Northamptons, who were outnumbered by three or four to one, if the 1st Queen's, who had been looking on from the right flank, suspecting foul play, had not promptly brought their machine-gun to bear on the situation. The 1st Coldstream were also quickly on the spot, and the German force was accounted for to a man.

Further west, in the Soupir district, the Guards' Brigade, who seemed specially singled out at this period for all the enemy's most ferocious attacks, were given a particularly bad time on this day. All attacks, however, were beaten off with severe loss to the enemy.

One incident is worth recording. North of Chavonne, where the 2nd Grenadiers were posted, there was a barn from which some snipers were keeping up a very irritating fire on the battalion. There was no artillery available at the moment for its destruction, and yet its destruction was of all things most desirable for the safety of the battalion. While the problem was under consideration, Corporal Thomas, of the 2nd Grenadiers, decided on a line of action. They were in a wheat-field in which the sheaves were stacked ready for carting. With a couple of comrades whom he persuaded to accompany him, he left the trenches, caught up a sheaf in each hand, and raced full tilt for the barn. There they piled up the sheaves against the wood-work, set fire to them and raced back again. Not a man of the party was touched, though both coming and going they ran through a hail of bullets. It is satisfactory to record that the barn burnt bravely and that the enemy retired with some rapidity. Later on, on November 6th, this same Grenadier, then a sergeant, gained the D.C.M. for another act of conspicuous gallantry.

The British force had now been five days on the Aisne, and had lost an average of 2,000 men per day. On the 17th, one of the 2,000 to fall for his country was Captain Wright, R.E. He was only a unit—one out of a host that fell; but he stands out, both on account of the manner of his death and because only a short three weeks before he had gained the Victoria Cross for great gallantry during the destruction of one of the bridges over the Mons canal. On this occasion the 5th C.B. had to get across to the south side of the river. Now that further advance was for the time being out of the question, the north side of the Aisne was clearly no place for cavalry. So the 5th C.B. had to get back across the pontoon bridge at Vailly. The bridge itself and both banks were under shell-fire, but Captain Wright, who was responsible for the bridge, considered himself equally responsible for the safety of those who crossed. The casualties among the cavalry were not many; but there were some; and it was while helping one of these wounded men into shelter that Captain Wright was killed.

On the night following, there was another gallant death among the Sappers. It was highly important to establish telephonic communication between the 9th Brigade on the north bank and Divisional headquarters on the south bank. There was no bridge and there was no boat. The river was swollen, sixty yards across and very uninviting. A private in the R.E. volunteered to try and swim across with a line; but he was a married man, and Lieutenant Hutton, R.E., would not allow it. He himself took the line, plunged into the river, and very nearly got across, but was sucked under by the eddies and drowned.

Another act this day which gained no Victoria Cross was that of Captain Everlegh, of the 52nd Oxford Light Infantry, who left the shelter of his trench to help a wounded animal, and was killed by a shell in so doing. It does not detract from the nobility of the act that the animal in question was only a pig.

The German attack was still mainly confined to the right end of our line, where the Germans ceaselessly, and always unsuccessfully, tried to drive the 1st A.C. from the heights on which they had established themselves in the first day's fighting. The Germans lost very heavily in these attacks and our own casualties were far from light. On the 20th the Aisne casualty list had mounted up to 561 officers and 13,000 men. In order to make up deficiencies, the C. in C. decided to send up the 18th Brigade, out of the 6th Division, just arrived, to support the 2nd Brigade on the extreme right of our line.

The 18th Brigade, on its arrival, took up a position between the 2nd Brigade and the French, with the W. Yorks as its right-hand battalion. It was this battalion's first day's fighting, and its initiation was a particularly cruel one, for the French troops, who should have protected its right, coolly went away to their dinner, leaving the flank of the W. Yorks absolutely unprotected, with the result that they found themselves mercilessly enfiladed and driven from their trenches with considerable loss. The Sherwood Foresters, also in the 18th Brigade, were in reserve down a steep slope in rear of the W. Yorks trenches. They were lying down in groups, talking over the prospects of their first day in the fighting line, when the news of the disaster above reached them. Without waiting to get into any formation, they jumped to their feet and charged up the slope. The officers were so far ahead as to be conspicuous, and nearly half of their number fell, but the survivors charged home, and, supported by some of the 4th Dragoon Guards, dismounted, led by Major Bridges, they joined up with the W. Yorks and re-took the lost trenches. The French, returning hurriedly from their dinner, full of apologies for their absence, and anxious to make reparation, put in some useful work with the bayonet on our flank.

This little affair cost us six hundred men, the Sherwood Foresters alone losing fourteen officers.

Between September 20th and 25th the battle of the Aisne seemed on the high road to die of inanition. It had come in like a lion; it went out like a very small lamb. When we use the term "battle of the Aisne" we are, of course, talking parochially. The Aisne battle has now been raging for an indefinite number of months over a front of a hundred miles. For us, however, the meaning of the term does not extend beyond the four weeks during which British and German troops faced one another between Soissons and Bourg. This is the only battle of the Aisne we are at present concerned with, and this battle began to get very quiet and uneventful. The weather, however, took a turn for the better, the wind shifting round out of the north-west, and sunshine once more took the place of the bitter rain storms of the past fortnight.

On the 25th, German activity was to some extent revived by the arrival of 200,000 reinforcements from Brussels and from the neighbourhood of Verdun. These came up by train by way of Liége and Valenciennes, and were distributed at various points along the enemy's right. The Verdun troops were reported very weary. The stimulus afforded by the arrival of these new troops was, however, merely sporadic, and from the point of view of public interest the Aisne battle may be said to have shot its bolt. Its waning days were, however, illuminated by one individual act of such remarkable courage that the history of the Aisne period would scarcely be complete without it.

On the morning of the 28th, while the 2nd Coldstream were

on the left of the 4th Brigade at what was known as the Tunnel post, the men of Captain Follett's company were sent out in a very thick mist to reconnoitre. It was a risky undertaking, for the German lines were very close. Suddenly the mist lifted, and two out of the three were instantly shot, the third getting home with only a graze. As leaving them where they lay meant fourteen hours' exposure before they could be got in under cover of darkness, Private Dobson volunteered to try and get them in at once. The undertaking appeared on the face of it an absolute impossibility, as it involved crossing a good deal of open ground in full view of the enemy. However, Dobson crawled out and managed to reach the men, one of whom he found dead, and the other wounded in three places. He applied first-aid dressings and then crawled back. A few minutes later he crawled out again, this time in company with Corporal Brown, the two men dragging a stretcher between them on which the wounded man was placed and dragged back into safety, none of the three being hit. It need scarcely be added that Dobson got the Victoria Cross for this most remarkable performance, Corporal Brown being awarded the D.C.M.

Towards the end of September operations in the Champagne country, as has been said, were beginning to stagnate. The Aisne had ceased to be a battlefield on which contending forces strove for position, and met in open shock on the downs, or in the beet fields. It had degenerated into a scene of mutual siege, where, in parallel lines of trenches, two armies were content to sit down and block progress. In view of the steady decrease in the distance between the hostile trenches, artillery operations had gradually assumed a more or less complimentary character and the game of war became restricted to sniping and construction work. With each succeeding day the position became more and more aggravated as trenches were made deeper and more secure, and entanglements of all kinds reduced still further the possibility of surprise or assault. For the soldier on duty such operations have but little interest; for the historian or the student of war they have none. We may, therefore, turn without reluctance to the more general situation, which by now was rapidly beginning to develop in interest.

The end of September and the beginning of October found both the Germans and the Allied Armies extending their flanks westward. As growing familiarity with the trench system of warfare began to make it clear to both sides that no further progress was possible by means of direct pressure, the German and Allied leaders began to scent a more favourable outlet for their energies on the western flank of operations, where—and where only—a roadway still lay open. The gradual shifting of German troops westward, or, to be more accurate, north-westward, could have no meaning but that of an attempt to force their way into France along the flat plains of Western Flanders; and no sooner was such an intention made plain than a corresponding movement was made by the Allies in an endeavour to forestall the enemy and envelop his flank before he could extend it. It was clear that the German move postulated the speedy capture of Antwerp, as the fall of that fortress was a necessary preliminary to any extended movement along the Belgian seaboard. A considerable British force was in process of being sent to Antwerp, and in addition to this force, the 7th Division and 3rd Cavalry Division were landed at Zeebrugge on October 7th, with a view to co-operating either with the Antwerp troops or with the main Allied army as circumstances dictated.

A consideration of these several important factors in the situation suggested to the C. in C. the desirability of entrusting the western extension movement, in the first instance, to the British Army at the moment occupying the Aisne trenches. Not only would such an exchange of positions greatly increase the facilities for bringing up supplies and for communications generally with England, but, in the event of the co-operation of the 7th and 3rd Cavalry Divisions, it would have the advantage of putting that detached body of troops in touch with the left of the main British army and so of consolidating the command.

General Joffre at first demurred, on account of the obvious objections attending the transfer from one set of troops to another of trenches situated so very close to those of the enemy as were ours on the Aisne, such transfer only being possible at night and under the strictest precautions. The C. in C, however, was insistent, and in the end the French General was persuaded that the advantages of the plan outweighed the drawbacks. There can be no question now but that the judgment of the C. in C. was fully endorsed by the event.

The transfer of troops was begun on October 3rd, on which day the cavalry set out by road for Flanders, and two days later the 2nd A.C. started entraining for St. Omer at Pont Ste. Maxence and Soissons. Nothing could have been more auspicious than the start of the cavalry as they turned their backs on the Aisne valley. The heavy rains of mid-September had been succeeded by a spell of magnificent weather, and on the morning of the 3rd it was at its best. The sun shone out of a clear sky, and, slanting over the backs of the men as they rode, fell full on the wooded slopes above Le Moncel and Chivres, where the tints of autumn were already beginning to show among the green. Below, down the valley, the winding Aisne showed up here and there, reflecting back the blue of the sky. The spirits of all ranks were in tune with the weather and the scene. Trench warfare offers no opportunities to cavalry— as cavalry—and the change westward at any rate carried with it the promise of increased action.

CHAPTER 17

Manoeuvring Westward

General Foch, with his headquarters at Doulens, at this time commanded all the French troops north of Noyon, and the Flanders plan of campaign was arranged between him and the C. in C. as follows: The 2nd A.C. was to occupy the canal line from Aire to Béthune, and the 3rd A.C. on arrival was to extend that line northward. The road running from Béthune to Lille was to be the dividing line between French and British, and the aim of the British force was to be to wheel to the right and so menace the flank of the Germans facing the 21st French Army Corps under General Maistre. The 7th Division and the 3rd Cavalry Division from Belgium were to co-operate in this general wheeling movement as circumstances permitted.

This scheme, as things turned out, was destined to be entirely upset by the fall of Antwerp on October 9th. For the first week it worked admirably, and the cavalry patrols and infantry outposts opposed to us fell back—as had been anticipated—before our advance. Then German reinforcements began to come up. Four Army Corps were railed up from the eastern frontier, to which were presently added some 90,000 troops released by the fall of Antwerp.

However, before these things happened, we had made some progress from our original line in an attempt to carry out the formulated scheme. On October 11th the detrainment of the 2nd A.C. was completed and Sir Horace moved his two divisions into position between Aire and Béthune. On October 12th the 3rd A.C, under General Pulteney, arrived at St. Omer and moved forward to Hazebrouck. The moment this army corps was in position Sir

Horace made the first move in the contemplated sweep by pushing forward the 3rd Division, which was on the left of the 2nd A.C, with orders to cross the Lawe Canal, which the enemy was reported to be holding in force. The advance was carried out with but little serious opposition, except in the neighbourhood of the locks at Etroa, where the 2nd R. Scots in the 8th Brigade met with a stubborn resistance, in the course of which Lieutenant Trotter was killed and Captain Croker (in command of the battalion) and Captain Heathcote badly wounded. The battalion, however, in spite of losses, continued to advance with great gallantry to the line of the canal, which Captain Tanner and Lieutenant Cazenove, with the leading company, eventually succeeded in crossing by the lock-gates, an exploit for which the former received the D.S.O. and the latter the Military Cross. The defenders thereupon at once gave way, suffering heavily in their retirement from the rifle fire of the 4th Middlesex on the right.

On the following morning the 3rd Division advance was renewed, the brigade chiefly concerned being once again the 8th, in the centre. This brigade set out at 6.30, the Middlesex being on the right, the R. Scots in the centre, and the 1st Gordon Highlanders on the left.

The country was dead flat, and the advance very slow owing to the innumerable water-dykes with which the country is intersected and which could only be crossed by means of planks or ladders borrowed from the farms.

About midday the Middlesex captured the village of Croix Barbée and the R. Scots performed the same office by Pont de Hem, but shortly afterwards further advance was checked, the enemy being found in considerable force and strongly entrenched, and the country offering no sort of cover. The brigade, however, though unable to advance, refused to retire, and very fierce fighting ensued, in the course of which the enemy made two most determined counter-attacks, one on Lieutenant Henderson's Company on the left of the R. Scots, and one on Captain Passy's Company on the left of the Middlesex line. Both these attacks were repulsed with heavy loss to the enemy, but the casualties on our side were also severe, Lieutenant Henderson—who was awarded the Cross of the Legion of Honour for the great gallantry which he displayed throughout these operations—being badly wounded, and Captain Passy's Company being reduced to the dimensions of a platoon. By nightfall the R. Scots had lost, during the day, 9 officers and close on 400 men. Second-Lieutenants Hewitt, Kerr and Snead-Cox had been killed, and of Captain Morrison's Company all the officers and 175 rank and file had been either killed or wounded.

The losses in the Middlesex were almost as severe, Lieutenant Coles, among others, being killed and Major Finch and Captain Passy severely wounded. Both battalions, however, maintained their ground with the utmost determination.

On the 14th some more of the actors in the approaching drama began to fall into their allotted places. The immortal 7th Division reached Ypres from Dixmude at midday and went into billets. The 3rd Cavalry Division arrived at the same time and from the same quarter, and split up, the 6th C.B. going to Wytschate and the 7th C.B. to Kemmel. The original Cavalry Brigades had now been re-organized, de Lisle taking over the 1st Division from Allenby, Gough retaining the second, and both divisions forming a "Cavalry Corps" under General Allenby. The 3rd Cavalry Division, on the other hand, had no part or parcel in this Cavalry Corps, being a separate and independent organization, under General the Hon. J. Byng.

During the day the Cavalry Corps captured the high ground above Béthune after some stiff fighting, while the 3rd A.C. advanced and occupied Bailleul, which was found to be full of German wounded. The 9th Brigade on the left of the 3rd Division was still pushing ahead, but the 8th Brigade was found to have got too far in advance of the troops further north, who had the bigger sweep to make, and General Doran, the Brigadier, ordered the brigade to entrench where it was, the R. Irish Regiment under Major Daniell being brought up from reserve to fill the gaps made the previous day in the ranks of the 4th Middlesex and 2nd R. Scots.

Sir Hubert Hamilton, the Divisional General, shortly afterwards came along on foot to inspect the trenches, disregarding warnings as to the great danger he was running. He proceeded on foot down the Richebourg Road, which was swept by shell-fire, in company with Captain Strutt, commanding the R. Scots, and was almost immediately killed by a shell, Captain Strutt being at the same time rendered unconscious. The General's A.D.C., Captain Thorp, ran forward and knelt by Sir Hubert's body, trying to screen it from the shells which were now falling thickly on the road. Captain Strutt shortly afterwards recovered consciousness, but was almost immediately severely wounded by another shell, and the command of the R. Scots devolved on Lieutenant Cazenove. This battalion had now lost 15 officers and over 500 men in the last three days' operations, but its casualties were to a certain extent repaired by the timely arrival of a draft of 180 men and several officers from home.

While the 3rd Division was thus pushing slowly ahead in the face of great natural difficulties, the 5th Division was being heavily engaged in the neighbourhood of Givenchy. Little forward progress was either asked for or expected from this division, the canal south of Givenchy having been, from the first, the selected pivot of the proposed wheeling movement. It was also a matter of common knowledge that the Germans were in far greater strength here than they were further north, the original idea of the wheeling movement having been, in fact, entirely based on the knowledge of the gradually diminishing strength of the German forces as they stretched northwards.

The first regiment to take a conspicuous part in the terrific fighting which for three weeks raged round Givenchy was the Dorsets. This was on the 13th, *i.e.*, on the same day on which the 8th Brigade made its advance to Croix Barbée and Pont de Hem.

It was a miserable day, foggy and wet. The Dorsets were on the extreme right of our army, in a line of trenches on the low ground between Givenchy and the canal. The attack was pressed with great vigour by the enemy, and the 1st Bedfords, on the left of the Dorsets, were driven out of the village of Givenchy. The left flank of the Dorsets was now exposed to enfilading fire from the ridge on which Givenchy stands, and their position was distinctly precarious. Some of the left-hand trenches were all but surrounded, the enemy having pressed forward into the gap at Givenchy, and from thence bearing down on the flank of the Dorsets. That regiment, however, held on with the utmost tenacity and successfully defended its position against repeated and most determined attacks; but the position was distinctly critical, and it was felt to be essential that orders of some sort should be received from Brigade headquarters. The telephonic communication had unfortunately been cut and there was no means of getting a message through except by hand, which, in the circumstances, seemed an all but impossible undertaking. A private of the name of Coombs, however, volunteered to try, and on the outward voyage actually got through untouched, but on returning with the necessary orders he was shot clean through the chest, but continued running for another 200 yards till he had delivered his message.

The orders received were that the Dorsets were to hold on, and this they continued to do, and with such good results that about 10 a.m. a long line of Germans was seen advancing with hands up and a white flag. The Dorsets left their trenches to accept this surrender and were instantly raked from end to end by concealed machine-guns from beyond the canal. These machine-guns had evidently been trained on the Dorsets' position in anticipation of that which actually happened, proving beyond any question that the whole thing was one carefully thought-out piece of treachery. The Dorsets being got fairly in line, and fully exposed to the concentrated fire of several machine-guns, literally fell in hundreds. Major Roper was killed and Colonel Bols was shot through the back and actually taken prisoner, but in the subsequent confusion he managed to crawl away and rejoin what was left of his battalion. The most unsatisfactory part of the whole affair was, that if the French Territorials on the south side of the canal, *i.e.*, on the right of the Dorsets, had been where they ought to have been, that which happened never could have happened; but instead of being up in line, for some unexplained reason they were a quarter of a mile behind.

The loss, however, was limited—as a loss—to the treacherous massacre of several hundred gallant men, and the capture of two of the supporting guns. The Gunners, as usual, behaved with the utmost gallantry, but they too came under the same enfilading fire as the Dorsets and every man of the detachment except Captain Boscawen fell either killed or wounded. Two of the guns were captured, but, with this, the material advantage gained by the enemy began and ended, for the 1st Cheshires were brought up from reserve and, with their co-operation, the morning's line was re-oc-cupied. The Cheshires, however, themselves suffered considerably, among their casualties being their C.O., Colonel Vandeleur, who was killed while leading the attack.[1]

On the 15th, as though in fury at the loss of their gallant General, the 3rd Division, now under the command of General Mackenzie, fought with a dash and determination which were irresistible. Their advance was continually checked by the country dykes, but, in spite of these hampering obstacles, the Germans were everywhere driven back with heavy loss. The 4th Middlesex and the 2nd R. Scots again did particularly good work, and, further north, in the 9th Brigade, the R. Fusiliers and the Northumberland Fusiliers gained high praise from the A.C. Commander for the vigour and activity with which they pushed forward in the face of strong opposition.

Conneau's cavalry, filling the eight-mile gap between the two Army Corps, also made good progress, as did the 3rd A.C., on the left. In the case of the latter Army Corps the 6th Division succeeded in reaching Sailly without encountering serious opposition, while the 4th Division got as far as Nieppe. The 2nd A.C., in its attempt to wheel, had so far advanced its left flank three miles in the last four days at a cost of 90 officers and 2,000 men. It had, however, inflicted very heavy losses on the enemy.

On the 16th the 3rd Division continued the wheeling movement with little opposition till it reached the village of Aubers, which was found to be strongly held, and where it was brought up short.

So much for the present as regards the general movement forward of the four divisions of infantry working south of Le Gheir. The attempt to drive the enemy back was destined to prove abortive, but this was not generally recognized by October 17th, and the idea was still to push our troops forward. This general desire to advance soon communicated itself to the 15th Brigade, on the extreme right of the British line at Givenchy, which had so far been looked upon as the pivot on which the left was to sweep round, and on the morning of the 17th the brigade was ordered to push

---

1. Colonel Vandeleur, while leading the Cheshires at Givenchy, was *not* killed as originally reported, but was wounded, fell into the hands of the Germans and finally escaped to England.

ahead. During the night of the 16th the 1st Devons had taken over the trenches just north of the canal in which the Dorsets had suffered such terrible casualties three days earlier. The 1st Bedfords were on their left, and on their right, of course, were the French Territorials south of the canal.

At 5 a.m. on the morning of the 17th a great bombardment was concentrated upon Givenchy, and the Germans were soon shelled out of that place, which had been in their possession since the 13th. A general advance was thereupon ordered.

As a precaution against the calamity which had overtaken the Dorsets, the Devons put one company on the south side of the canal. This company was in touch with the French Territorials—so long as these latter kept up in line, which, as it proved, was not for long. The advance was made under considerable difficulties, as the country afforded no natural cover, and the enemy was found to be in far greater force than had been anticipated. However, in spite of a most continued and stubborn resistance, the Devons, in obedience to orders, succeeded in advancing their position 1,000 yards, and held on there till dusk, waiting for the French Territorials on their right and the regiment on their left to come up into line. These, however, failed to arrive, and it soon became clear that for the Devons to remain isolated at the point to which they penetrated could only result in the capture of the entire battalion. Their retirement, however, in the circumstances, was a matter of extreme difficulty, the country being quite flat and entirely destitute of cover. The enemy were favoured by an exceptionally clear field for their fire, and all their attention was naturally focussed on the one battalion which had dared to push so far ahead. The men were sheltering as best they could in ditches and behind haystacks, of which there was fortunately a fair sprinkling. When the order came to retire some crept away under shelter of the hedges; others had not even this cover, and had to take their chance in the open.

One detachment of some forty men were sheltering behind a large haystack in the open. They were quickly located, and shrapnel and machine-gun fire was concentrated on the haystack, which soon began to dwindle under the hail of missiles. Lieutenant Worrall, who was one of the party, thereupon set fire to the haystack, and told the men to make a bolt for it singly, under cover of the smoke. This they successfully did, and with few further casualties—all but Sergeant Harris and another man, who were wounded and could not move. The haystack was now beginning to blaze fiercely and it was clear the men could not be left. Lieutenant Worrall picked up Sergeant Harris and carried him 400 yards across the open to the shelter of the canal bank, where he left him. Then he went back for the other man.

In the meanwhile the line further north was still making a certain progress. At Lorgies a party of the K.O.S.B. Cyclists, under Corporal Wheeler, rode right into the enemy outposts. They promptly dismounted, and, opening fire, held the enemy for half an hour till the brigade (the 13th) arrived on the scene and captured the place. Still further north again General Shaw and his 9th Brigade was as usual fairly active. About 4 p.m. the R. Scots Fusiliers and the Northumberland Fusiliers attacked and carried the village of Aubers with the bayonet, completely routing the occupying troops; and a little later the R. Fusiliers and Lincolns performed the same office by the village of Herlies.

Aubers stands on the crest of the ridge which faces Neuve Chapelle. Herlies, on the other hand, lies at the foot of a long, gradual slope of open, cultivated land. The village was defended on the west side by a semi-circular line of trenches, protected by barbed wire entanglements. The defenders had also a Horse Artillery Battery and—as usual—a great number of machine-guns posted here and there in any suitable buildings. The two attacking battalions, on the other hand, were supported by a R.F.A. battery and a section of howitzers. These did admirable preliminary work, and at dusk the two regiments—Lincolns on right, R. Fusiliers on left—charged the trenches, carried them hot-handed and pursued the Germans into the village. Here further pursuit was unfortunately checked by the too great activity of our own artillery, but the position won was occupied and held for six days. The Lincolns, who were the chief sufferers, lost seventy-five men and two officers during this attack.

Further north, Conneau's cavalry added their share to the day's work by capturing Fromelles, so that there was an appreciable advance all round, which would have been greater still had not the 7th Brigade, which was on the right of the 3rd Division, failed to take the village of Illies.

The position then at night on the 17th was that the pivot point remained on the canal, south of Givenchy. From that point the line of the 2nd A.C. curved round behind La Bassée and through Violaines, after which it zigzagged towards the north-east in an irregular salient, the 3rd A.C. being thrown back on its left.

Such was still the state of things on the morning of the 18th, when the Germans—having been reinforced during the night by the XIII. Division of the VII. Corps—made counter-attacks all along the line of the 2nd A.C. All these were repulsed with loss to the enemy, but our own line made no advance, the stumbling-block being still Illies, which continued to defy capture by the 7th Brigade.

At dusk the undefeated 9th Brigade stormed and took the trenches one mile north-east of Illies, but as they were unsupported on either flank, they had to abandon the position and fall back. The 1st R. Scots Fusiliers did particularly good work on this occasion, and suffered correspondingly, Captain Burt and Lieutenants Cozens-Brooke, the Hon. J. Doyle, and Fergusson-Barton being killed, and six other officers wounded. In the meanwhile Conneau had advanced from Fromelles and attacked Fournes, but this attack failed.

Meanwhile, in the Armentières district, the 3rd A.C. was making great efforts to play up to its allotted part in the wheel to the south, the 4th Division being north of Armentières, the 6th Division south of it. The centre of interest was still to the south of Armentières, the concentration of German troops north of that town being still only in process of development. For the moment, then, we can neglect affairs further north, and follow the attempted wheeling movement of the troops south of Armentières to its furthest point east.

On the afternoon of the 18th the 16th Brigade captured Radinghem, the two battalions chiefly concerned being the 2nd Lancs. and Yorks. and the 1st Buffs. These two battalions, who were on the right of the 6th Division, gallantly stormed and carried the village and then—in the impetuosity of success and enterprise—followed on beyond after the retreating Germans. Here, in pushing forward through an impenetrable wood, they suddenly found themselves swept from all sides by concealed machine-guns, which literally rained bullets on them. The casualties here were very high, the Lancs. and Yorks. alone losing 11 officers and 400 men. Colonel Cobbold and Major Bailey, however, who displayed the greatest coolness and courage throughout, succeeded in withdrawing the remains of the battalion in good order and getting it back to Radinghem.

The two battalions, in spite of their heavy losses, retained possession of this village throughout the night, though—had the Germans counter-attacked in force—things might have gone badly with them, as they were two miles ahead of the rest of the division.

CHAPTER 18

From Attack to Defence

It was now generally recognized that the wheeling movement originally contemplated was an impossibility. Between Armentières and Givenchy the 3rd, 5th, and 6th Divisions, and Conneau's cavalry, which was acting with them, had opposed to them the II., IV., VII. and IX. German Cavalry Divisions, several battalions of Jägers, the XIII. Division of the VII. A.C., a brigade of the III. A.C., and the whole of the XIV. A.C., which had recently moved north from in front of the 21st French Army. They were therefore sufficiently outnumbered, even at this period, to put any idea of further advance quite out of the question. It now became merely a matter of holding on to that which they had got—if possible.

The 2nd A.C. front, owing to the irregularity of the advance, was of a zigzag character, and on the night of the 19th Sir Horace ordered a slight retirement so as to straighten out the line. It was quickly evidenced that this step was not taken a moment too soon, for on the following day the Germans, confident in the sufficiency of their numbers, attacked all along the line, and succeeded in recapturing Le Pilly, and with it the whole of the R. Irish Regiment. This was something of a disaster, but luckily the attack was not equally successful elsewhere. The 1st Cheshires, though attacked with great vigour, held their ground unshaken throughout this day and the next, and inflicted heavy loss on the enemy. Two platoons of the R. Fusiliers, who were sent up to establish communication between Herlies and the R. Irish Regiment at Le Pilly, were caught in flank, owing to the capture of the latter place, and suffered severely, Captain Carey, in command, being killed.

The 9th Brigade, which had throughout these operations been on the left of the 3rd Division, was now temporarily transferred to the 3rd A.C., whose line, reaching as it did from Radinghem to Le Gheir, was considered by the C. in C. to be too thin for safety. The removal of this brigade had the effect of widening the gap between the 2nd and 3rd A.Cs by a further four or five miles, and the responsibilities of Conneau's cavalry were correspondingly increased, the left of the 2nd A.C. now stopping short at Riez, which was held by the 1st Gordons. The weakening of the 2nd A.C. by the borrowing of one of its brigades and the capture of one of its battalions was made up to it in some measure by the arrival of the Lahore Division of Indians, under General Watkis, which took up a position in rear of it at Neuve Chapelle.

With the additional assistance which had been lent him, General Pulteney was everywhere successful in holding his ground. At one moment in the day the enemy succeeded in getting possession of Le Gheir, but as the loss of this place would have laid bare the flank of the cavalry at St. Yves, General Hunter-Weston decided that it must be retaken at any cost, and the work was entrusted to the K.O. Regiment and the Lancs. Fusiliers. These two battalions, finely handled by Colonel Butler, of the Lancs. Fusiliers, proved themselves quite equal to the call made upon them, and not only re-captured the lost trenches, but took 200 prisoners and released 40 of our own men who had been captured.

CHAPTER 19

The Birth of the Ypres Salient

It is necessary now to turn for the moment to the scene further north, where a mild interest was beginning to be displayed
in England in the war-clouds which were gathering round the
picturesque and historical Flemish town of Ypres. It will be remembered that, on the 14th, Sir Henry Rawlinson, with the 7th
Division and the 3rd Cavalry Division, had reached Ypres from
Dixmude. On their first arrival, the 3rd Cavalry Division had been
sent south of Ypres, the 6th C.B. going to Wytschate and the 7th
C.B. to Kemmel; but as the cavalry corps under General Allenby
gradually drew up from the direction of Béthune, the 6th and 7th
C.B. (3rd Cavalry Division) were withdrawn to the north side of
Ypres, where they worked the ground between Zonnebeke and
the Forêt d'Houlthust, filling, in fact—as well as might be—the
gap between the French cavalry to the north and the left of the
7th Division. This latter division, since its arrival, had pushed forward with little or no opposition to a convex position some six
miles east of Ypres, which embraced the villages of Zonnebeke,
Kruiseik and Zandvoorde. South of Zandvoorde there was a considerable hiatus, Allenby's cavalry corps, which had unexpectedly
found itself opposed by the XIX. Saxon Corps and three divisions
of German cavalry, having not yet got into proper touch with the
right of the 7th Division. This, however, in view of the fact that
the 7th Division was on the outside of the wheeling movement,
and had therefore the bigger sweep to make, was a matter of little
moment, and one which would have speedily righted itself at a
later stage, had the original plan been successfully carried through.

A matter of more moment at the time was that the 22nd Brigade, on the left of the 7th Division at Zonnebeke, was considerably in arrear of the 20th Brigade at Kruiseik, whereas the converse should have been the case. Accordingly, in the early morning of the 19th, the 22nd Brigade was ordered to advance from Zonnebeke in the direction of the straight road connecting Roulers and Menin, so as to bring the left shoulder of the 7th Division well forward. When this had been done, the 20th and 21st Brigade were to join in the general advance.

The main idea on the extreme left of our line, at the moment, was to seize the bridge over the River Lys at Menin, and so impede the further advance of the German reinforcements which were being steadily railed up from the direction of Lille. In the event it turned out that the manoeuvre was impracticable owing to the insufficiency in numbers of the British force operating east of Ypres. This force, it will be understood, consisted, at the time, of the 7th Division alone, supported by two cavalry brigades on its left flank, whereas the Germans had by the 19th concentrated on the spot a force of five or six times this magnitude. However, in the intention lies the explanation of the subsequent Ypres salient. The original idea was strategically sound, but it was frustrated owing to the difficulty and consequent delay in concentration which accompanied the transfer of the British force from the Aisne to its new field of operation in Flanders. It was a race as to which army could concentrate with the greatest rapidity, and the Germans—having by far the easier task and by far the shorter road to travel—got in first.

At 5 a.m., then, on the 19th, the 22nd Brigade set out from Zonnebeke on its forward movement, the 2nd Queen's on the left, the 1st R. Welsh Fusiliers in the centre, and the 2nd Warwicks on the right, the 1st S. Staffords being in reserve.

This 22nd Brigade, as it turned out, was the only one in the 7th Division which was destined to do any fighting this day. The 20th Brigade, which was at Kruiseik, some couple of miles in advance of the 22nd, never really came into action. As a matter of fact, they were in the act of deploying for an attack on Ghelowe about 11 a.m., when news was brought by an airman that two fresh German army corps had suddenly made their appearance, moving up from the direction of Courtrai. As far as this brigade was con-

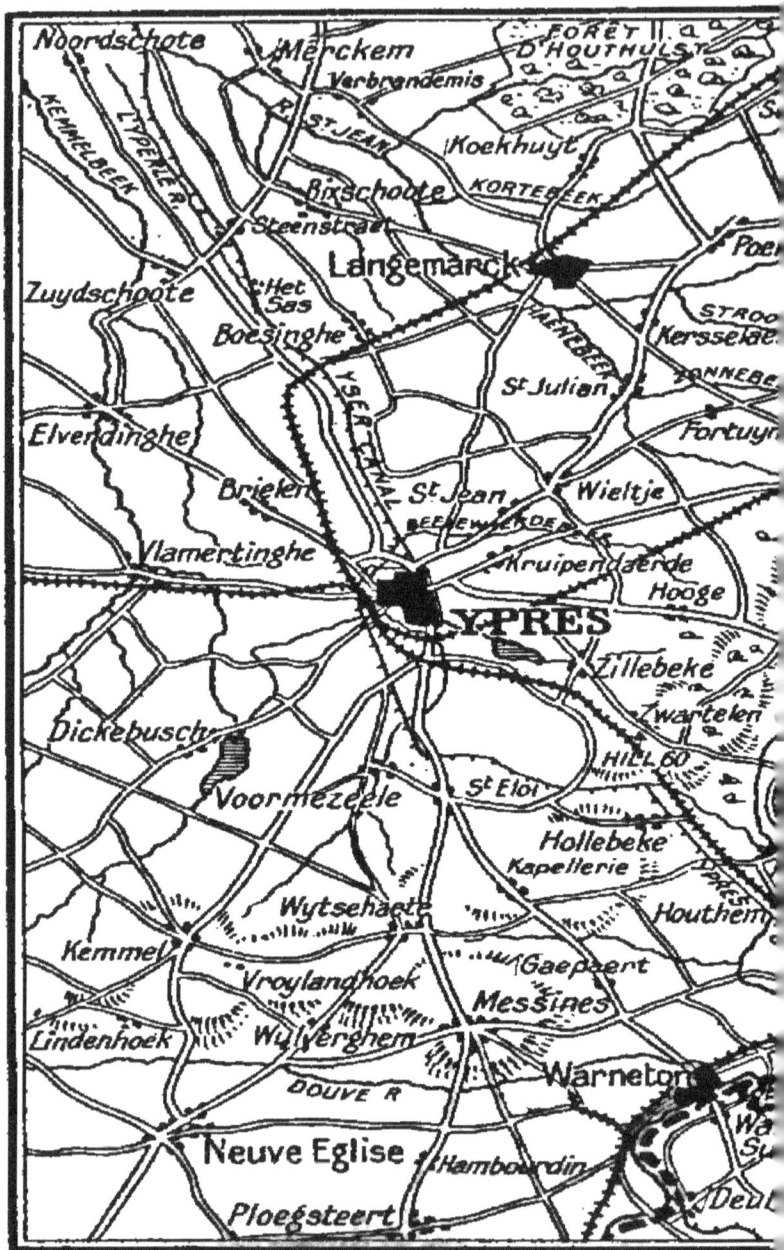

Ypres and its surroundings.

ROULERS

Schaap Baillie
Schierveld
Oostnieuwkerke
WESTROOSEBEKE
De Ruiter
St Eloi
Kasteelhoek
Magermerie
elcappelle
Mosselmarkt
Koekuythoek
Den Plas
Passchendaele
MOORSLEDE
Koolbrandershoek
Nieuwmalen
Snosekot
St Pieter
Keyberg
Stypskapelle
ZONNEBEKE
Oosthoek
Potteryebrug
Ledeghem
Noord Westhoek
DADIZEELE
Becelaere
Veldhoek
Terhard
Kezelberg
Zuydhoek
Pannemolen
GHELUVELT
Koelberg
Kleythoek
Kruistik
GHELUWE
Zandvoorde
America
Comenenhoek
Klytmolen
MENIN
Kortewilde
Tenbrielen
Coucou
WERVICQ
HALLUIN
Wervicq Sud
R.LYS
CANAL
Bousbecque
RONCQ
Bas Warneton
COMINES
Le Blaton
R.LYS
Warneton Sud et Bas
Marliere
Timborne
ulemont
Ste Barbe
LINSELLES

Railways shown thus:
Canals   "   "
Roads   "   "

cerned, then, the original order to advance was cancelled, it being clearly impracticable for one division to take the offensive against four. By this time, however, the 22nd Brigade had advanced some six miles from Zonnebeke to the neighbourhood of the straight road and the parallel railway which connect Roulers and Menin. The news of the unexpected reinforcement of the enemy in front was duly communicated to General Lawford, commanding the brigade, and he at once ordered the retirement of his four battalions. This order reached the Queen's and the Warwicks about 11.30, but did not penetrate through to the R. Welsh Fusiliers, who accordingly pressed on towards Ledeghem, quite ignorant of the new development, or of the fact that they were unsupported by the battalions on either flank. Ledeghem was found to be very strongly occupied, and on reaching the high road from Roulers to Menin, just short of the railway, the battalion found itself not only attacked in force from in front, but at the same time enfiladed from the direction of the main road on the left, and very heavily shelled from Keselburg on the right front. To this artillery fire there was no response whatever from our own gunners, who, it is to be presumed, were in ignorance of the single-handed advance of the R. Welsh Fusiliers, and had withdrawn with the rest of the brigade. The German artillery accordingly had it all its own way, and their shrapnel played havoc in the ranks of the gallant Welshmen. Nine officers[1] had already fallen when at 1.20 the order to retire reached the C.O. The order now was that the battalion was to withdraw to a ridge in rear, near the windmill at Dadizeele, and there act rear-guard to the rest of the brigade. This order was carried out without any great further loss, the enemy showing no disposition at the moment to advance, and eventually the brigade reached Zonnebeke in the dusk of the evening.

Throughout that night a constant stream of refugees passed through Zonnebeke on their way westward from Roulers, which was burning. These were all subjected to examination, but their number was too great to make close examination possible, and that many spies got through among them is unquestionable.

---

1. In this engagement Captain Kingston, Captain Lloyd, Captain Brennan and Lieutenant Chance were killed, and Major Gabbett, Captain St. John, Captain Skaife and Lieutenants Jones and Naylor were wounded.

It very soon became apparent that the newly-arrived German troops had no intention of letting the grass grow under their feet. During the night they had put behind them the six miles which separate Ledeghem from Zonnebeke, and at eleven o'clock on the morning of the 20th they started bombarding the latter place. Once more fate elected that the R. Welsh Fusiliers should stand in the path of the attack. They were now on the left of the 22nd Brigade, and they were attacked not only from the direction of the road, but from their left flank, which was very much exposed, the line of the cavalrymen north of the road being even more extended than that of the 7th Division. However, in spite of everything, they held their ground with great determination throughout this day and the next. Their losses, however, were again very severe indeed. This was, in fact, the first of the 7th Division battalions to undergo that gradual process of annihilation which was destined in time to be the fate of all. The extreme tension of the situation at Zonnebeke was in some part relieved by the arrival on the scene, during the night, of the 4th (Guards) Brigade, who took over the ground north of the Zonnebeke road from the cavalry. This brigade formed part of the 1st A.C. which had arrived at St. Omer from the Aisne on the 17th and 18th, and had been billeted outside Ypres on the night of the 19th.

The question as to how best to dispose of this 1st A.C. was an extremely delicate one. The numerical weakness of the Cavalry Corps, holding the Wytschate and Messines line, suggested strongly that it would be of the greatest use in that area. On the other hand was the very grave danger of the Allies' left flank being turned by the sudden advance of fresh German forces north and east of Ypres, of sufficient strength to break through the very thin line guarding that quarter. In this dilemma, the C. in C., with consummate judgment, decided to send Sir Douglas Haig's army corps to the northern side of Ypres. The wisdom of this step became apparent on the very next day, that is on the day when the 22nd Brigade advanced to the Roulers-Menin road, and were forced back by the unexpected appearance of two army corps whose presence was unknown to our air-scouts. These fresh German forces as we have seen, pursued the 22nd Brigade as far as Zonnebeke, and there attacked our line with the utmost determination on the 20th and

21st. On the first of these two days, the brigade, as already described, managed to hold its own—though at great sacrifice—but the German attacking force was all the time being augmented, while our defensive force, owing to continuous losses, was getting weaker; and it is hardly conceivable that the enemy's advance could have been checked for another twenty-four hours, except for the timely arrival of the 1st A.C.

As soon as the destination of this corps had been decided on between the C. in C. and Sir Douglas Haig, the latter hurried forward the Guards' Brigade to the assistance of the 7th Division, and these—as has already been explained—came up into line on the left of the R. Welsh Fusiliers on the night of the 20th, and were unquestionably very largely instrumental in preventing something in the nature of a *débâcle* on the 21st.

On that morning the enemy renewed the attack in great force at daybreak, and kept up a succession of violent assaults till four in the afternoon. The Welsh Fusiliers were again in the very path of the attack, but the presence of the Guards' Brigade on their left, north of the Zonnebeke road, just made the difference. With this backing, they successfully held out from daybreak till 4 p.m., by which time their trenches had been wholly annihilated and a retirement became necessary. Their difficulties were increased by the giving out of their ammunition, but the situation was to some extent saved by the gallantry of Sergeant-Drummer Chapman, who brought up fresh supplies under a very heavy fire. Another Welsh Fusilier who won great distinction during the day was Private Blacktin, who was awarded the D.C.M. for the continued heroism with which he attended to the wounded throughout the two days' fighting. Of these there were now, unfortunately, only too many, the Welsh Fusiliers having—in three successive days' fighting—lost 23 officers and 750 men. Their retirement in the evening was assisted by the 2nd Queen's, who (with the exception of one company, which was away to the right, supporting the Northumberland Hussars between the 22nd and 21st Brigade) were in the second line. This battalion too suffered severely during the operations, Lieutenants Ingram and Ive being killed, and Major Whinfield, Lieutenants Heath, Haigh, Williams and Gabb wounded. They effectively, however, checked the further advance of the enemy. By a piece of good fortune the S. Staffords, on the right of the Welsh Fusiliers, were also in a position to give the advancing Germans a very bad time. They had a body of expert shots posted in the upper windows of St. Joseph's school, from which point of vantage they were able to get the Germans in flank. The school was being shelled all the time, but was not hit. During the night which followed, however—a night of exceptional darkness—the Germans found an opportunity of pushing forward round the left flank of the S. Staffords, but without succeeding in dislodging them, till an order arrived at four o'clock in the morning for their retirement, as they were ahead of the line.

In the meanwhile the Guards' Brigade, north of the road, had not been idle, and it is not too much to say that, except for the arrival of this brigade in the very nick of time, the position would have been very nearly desperate. As it was, however, their presence at once made itself felt. The fire of the S. Staffords from the right, the Guards' Brigade from the left, and the 2nd Queen's from in face, was more than the German advance was prepared at the moment to push forward against, and it came to a standstill. The Guards' casualties were considerable, especially in the case of the 3rd Coldstream, who had the Hon. C. Monck and Lieutenant Waller killed, and Colonel Feilding, Lieutenant Darrell and Lieutenant Leese wounded. Lord Feilding was given the D.S.O. for conspicuous gallantry on this occasion. The 52nd Oxford Light Infantry, acting with the Guards' Brigade, proved in every way worthy of the association, and fully lived up to its great fighting reputation. Amongst those who particularly distinguished themselves in this regiment during the fight were Lieutenant Spencer, Corporal Hodges and Private Hastings.

In the events of these three days is to be found the origin of the singular bulge, or—in military parlance—salient, which throughout October characterized the disposition of our forces east of Ypres. By the unexpected appearance to our front of 80,000 fresh German troops, our contemplated progress eastward had perforce to be replaced, on the spur of the moment, by a grim determination to hold on as long as possible to the ground we had already won. This was, no doubt, a natural desire, but its fruit was unsound.

On the evening of October 21st the position was that the

21st Brigade at Becelaere and the 20th at Kruiseik and Zandvoorde were still very considerably ahead of the 22nd, which, as we have seen, had been driven back to Zonnebeke. North of Zonnebeke the line of the 1st Division fell still further back, facing, in fact, very nearly due north, while south of Zandvoorde there was no line at all, the 7th Division here ending in space, for reasons already given. Later on the 3rd Cavalry Division—when released from its duties north of Zonnebeke—were detailed for the duty of keeping up the communication between Zandvoorde and the cavalry corps far back at Hollebeke, Wytschate and Messines, but even so, the line they occupied fell back almost at right angles from our true front, and was a constant source of anxiety. For a General voluntarily to relinquish ground already won is probably the supreme act of renunciation, at the same time it is obvious that three sides of a square are longer than the fourth side, and therefore require more men for their defence, and it is no exaggeration to say that between October 20th and 26th the Ypres salient bore a perilous resemblance to three sides of a square.

The timely arrival of the 1st A.C. had undoubtedly saved the situation for the moment, as far as the German attempt to break through at Zonnebeke was concerned, but the position was still one for the very gravest anxiety. Even with the addition of the 1st A.C. we had only three infantry divisions and two cavalry brigades with which to defend the entire front from Bixschoote, due north of Ypres, to Hollebeke, nearly due south of it. From Bixschoote to Hollebeke, as the crow flies, is a matter of some eight miles, but, as our front at that time jutted out as far as Becelaere, six miles east of Ypres, it may be reckoned that the frontage to be defended was not less than sixteen miles in length. The strength of the enemy—that is to say, of the force which was immediately pressing forward at this moment on the Ypres frontage—may be approximately reckoned at 100,000; and had the German general at this juncture pushed his forces along all the main avenues to Ypres, it is difficult to see how he could have been held back. The line of defence was ridiculously extended—extended indeed far beyond the recognized limits of effective resistance, and there were no reserves available with which to strengthen any threatened spot. Every fighting man was in the long, thin line that swept round in that uncomfortable curve from Bixschoote to Hollebeke. The 89th French Territorial Division was, it is true, in general reserve, at Poperinghe, but this division was composed entirely of untried troops who could in no sense claim to be comparable to the French regulars. The 87th French Territorial Division, again, had as much as it could do to attend to its own affairs north of Ypres, and was not to be counted on as a source of reinforcement.

From this time on, the whole of our line north of the Zonnebeke road was gradually taken over by the 1st A.C., the 6th and 7th C.B., who had so far been responsible for that section of the front, being thereby released and retiring to Hooge, from which point, for the time being, they acted as a kind of mobile reserve— the fan-like arrangement of roads which branches out eastward from Ypres enabling them to be sent with the least possible delay to any threatened point on the front.

For purposes of descriptive clearness, it may perhaps be pardonable, even at the risk of labouring the point a little, to call attention once more to the fact that the British force in Flanders now consisted of two distinct and separate armies, which we may call the North and South Army. The South Army was made up of the 2nd A.C., the 3rd A.C., and the 19th Brigade, and was supported by Conneau's cavalry, which operated between these two army corps, and by the Lahore Indians in rear. The line of this army extended as far north as Le Gheir, or, rather, let us say, Ploegsteert, to which place the left of the 3rd A.C. shortly withdrew.

The North Army consisted of the 1st A.C. and the 7th Division, supported by the 3rd Cavalry Division, and the southernmost point in its charge at the moment was Hollebeke, or, to be more precise, the canal which turns off sharply towards Ypres just north of Hollebeke. The eight miles gap between the North Army and the South Army was held by the cavalry corps under Allenby.

The terrific fighting, then, of the end of October and beginning of November may be considered as taking place in three distinct sections, viz.—the South Army, the Cavalry Corps, and the North Army. The latter, it may be added, had the 89th French Territorial

Division in support, and General Bidon, with the 87th French Territorial Division, on its left, north of Ypres.

The fact that the 1st A.C. had arrived on the scene absolutely at the psychological moment in order to avert disaster, was made abundantly clear, not only by the effective support which the 2nd Division of that army corps was able to lend north of the Zonnebeke road on the 21st, but also by the immediate demand which arose further south for the services of the released 3rd Cavalry Division. These two cavalry brigades, it will be remembered, had been replaced on the night of the 20th by the 2nd Division, who had taken over their position north of the Zonnebeke road.

At 1 p.m. on the following day, that is, at the same time that the Welsh Fusiliers were being so fiercely attacked along the Zonnebeke road, news arrived that Gough's 2nd Cavalry Division was being very hard pressed, and had been forced to fall back on Messines. This left a gap, or—to be more accurate—widened the gap on the right of the 7th Division at Zandvoorde, and the 6th C.B. (10th Hussars, Royals, and 3rd Dragoon Guards) were sent off to fill it, as well as might be, by occupying the two canal crossings north of Hollebeke. This they did with success, and the 10th Hussars and 4th Hussars (from the 3rd C.B.) even attacked the Château de Hollebeke itself, but were unable to take it, on account of its being still under fire from our own artillery. Later on in the evening, however, it was felt that the line south-west of Zandvoorde was dangerously open, and the 6th C.B. was shifted in that direction, the 10th Hussars at 3 o'clock in the morning taking over the Zandvoorde trenches from the 2nd Scots Guards in the 20th Brigade. The 7th C.B. went into reserve at St. Eloi, where it remained for the night. In the meanwhile the C. in C. had sent up the 7th Indian Brigade to help support Gough.

This transfer of the Zandvoorde trenches into the keeping of the 3rd Cavalry Division was the first abridgement of the immense frontage (from Zonnebeke to south of Zandvoorde) held by the 7th Division. From this time on, till the moment when they were permanently abandoned, it will be found that these Zandvoorde trenches were in the occupation either of the 6th C.B. or the 7th C.B. They formed the most dangerous position in the whole line of defence, being in the form of a promontory which jutted out defiantly into the enemy's country. The 3rd Cavalry Division suffered very severely during its nine days' defence of these deadly trenches, the 10th Hussars, who were perhaps the worst sufferers, losing on the very first day of occupation Colonel Barnes, Major Mitford and Captain Stewart.

CHAPTER 20

The Stand of the
Fifth Division[1]

In the meanwhile, further south, at and around Givenchy, a situation was developing which in point of dramatic interest, and as a test of indomitable resolution, bid fair to rival the defence of Ypres. From Givenchy to Le Gheir the 2nd and 3rd A.C. had now definitely assumed the defensive, and the story of how that defence was maintained in the face of overwhelming odds, and under conditions of extreme difficulty and fatigue, is one of which Britain may ever be justly proud.

The 21st French Army was, throughout these La Bassée operations, responsible for the ground up to the canal south of Givenchy. From that point the 5th Division took up the line; then came the 3rd Division, then the 6th, and finally, with its left resting on Le Gheir, the 4th Division. Behind the 5th and 3rd Divisions were the Indians. Between Le Gheir and Zandvoorde, which we may take as the southernmost point of the arm of Ypres, was Allenby's Cavalry Corps.

In the case of the South Army, as with the Army of Ypres, the impetus of the first advance had carried our troops to a line which was only afterwards maintained under great strain, in the face of the masses of troops which the enemy were gradually concentrating in this particular area. La Bassée and Ypres became, for the time being, the two points on which German attention was specially riveted. With the avowed intention of breaking through to Calais by one or other of these routes, troops were being systematically

---

1. 13th, 14th and 15th Brigades.

railed up from the east and massed along the Belgian frontier. It was officially computed that by October 20th there were 250,000 German troops north of La Bassée, and that by the middle of November that number had been increased to 750,000.

The fact that it was the British army which stood between this vast mass of armed men and its projected advance was in all probability not entirely a matter of chance. If the attempt to break through either at Ypres or La Bassée had succeeded, the little British force would either have been wiped out, or hopelessly disgraced in the eyes of its allies. In either case the prestige of England would have received a rude shock; and, with a German base established at Calais, she would have been in imminent danger of losing something more than prestige.

The fact, then, that the Kaiser's selected road to Calais or Paris, as the case might be, lay through the thirty miles of front held by the British troops, was in all probability part of a carefully-thought-out plan. One factor in the case, however, had been overlooked, or at least under-rated, *viz.*—the indomitable tenacity of the British soldier in the face of difficulties. Of this essentially British quality the Germans had as yet had no practical experience. At Mons and Le Cateau we had dropped back before their onslaughts—dropped back, it is true, in obedience to orders, and in conformity with a pre-arranged plan. Still, we had dropped back. At the Aisne there had been no serious attempt on the part of the enemy to break through our lines. Such had not been part of the German programme at the moment. It was therefore not wholly unnatural, that the very thin British line between Givenchy and Ypres, should have been reckoned at German headquarters as being penetrable at any point where sufficient pressure was brought to bear.

In the face of beliefs such as these, the stone-wall resistance put up by our three war-worn army corps must have been a source of equal astonishment and exasperation to the wire-pullers in Berlin. To the Britisher it must always bring a thrill of justifiable pride. Many of the regiments engaged were technically "annihilated." Their officers went; their senior N.C.Os went; they were worn to the last stage of mental and physical exhaustion by sleeplessness, and by unceasing digging and fighting. And still they held on. There were no "hands uppers" among these men from Britain. We gave ground, of course, both in the La Bassée area and at Ypres. In the latter case a withdrawal of some kind was dictated by every consideration of military prudence. The original bulge was a danger from every point of view, and with no compensating advantage. It thinned our line and laid us open at all times to the risk of enfilading attacks from north and south.

At La Bassée, too, we had got too far ahead, and from the military point of view we lost nothing by falling back a few miles. But from the three points in the line of vital strategical importance, Givenchy, Ploegsteert and Klein Zillebeke, we were never driven. Those points were held on to with a stubborn determination which nothing could break through; and to the battalions on whose shoulders fell the main weight of this burden is due the homage of all who stayed at home. It is not suggested that there was an entirely uniform standard of excellence throughout all the units engaged. Any attempt to make such a representation would be a gross injustice to those battalions which stand out, and which have for ever immortalized themselves, and the honour of British arms, by an indomitable resistance which can find few parallels in the history of war.

But at first we got too far ahead at La Bassée as at Ypres, and this soon became very clear. During a thick fog on the morning of the 21st, some of the 5th Division were driven out of their trenches; and in lieu of making any attempt to retake the trenches so lost, General Morland—who on Sir Charles Fergusson's promotion had taken over command of the division—thought it advisable to readjust the entire line.

Further north, just east of Fromelles, the 19th Brigade had also to give ground. They fought all through this day with great gallantry, but their losses were very heavy, and, in spite of all efforts, by evening they had been forced back over a mile. The Argyll and Sutherland Highlanders were specially conspicuous on this occasion; they fought with indomitable valour, and it was only with the greatest reluctance that in the end they obeyed the order to abandon their trenches. In Sergeant Ross's platoon eighty per cent. had been killed or wounded, but the gallant sergeant still refused to give way.

This succession of small reverses was, of course, disappointing in view of the anticipations of the week before, but they brought home to all concerned a thorough realization of the change of outlook. This was still further emphasized by the shifting northwards of the 3rd A.C., a step which was rendered necessary by the obvious inadequacy of the cavalry corps numbers for the frontage allotted to it. By this move that frontage was appreciably shortened, but the gap between the 2nd and 3rd A.C. was correspondingly widened, and the difficulty of Conneau's gallant but highly tried corps of cavalry was proportionately increased. The effect on the Frenchmen was at once felt, these being driven out of Fromelles on the following afternoon with very heavy loss. On the same afternoon the 5th Division again suffered severely. The Cheshires were driven out of Violaines, and the Dorsets—terribly thinned though they had been by the fighting of the 13th—seeing them hard pressed, left their trenches and dashed up in support, but the odds were too heavy and both were driven back with loss. The Germans thereupon occupied Rue du Marais, a little village on the northern slope of the Givenchy ridge, but their advantage was short-lived, for they were promptly counter-attacked by the Manchesters and Worcesters and driven out again.

In the meanwhile the Devons had been forced to fall back some two miles from Canteleux, which they had now occupied for three days, to Givenchy, the former place having been formed into an untenable salient by the withdrawal of the troops on either flank.

In the evening General Morland told Sir Horace that the 5th Division was completely worn out with constant digging and fighting, and that he doubted whether they could withstand another attack. The 2nd A.C. had already in the last ten days lost 5,000 men, to which the 5th Division had contributed more than its share. This division had, in fact, from first to last had a most trying time. It had borne the brunt of the fighting at Le Cateau, and at the Aisne it had struck what proved to be by far the most difficult crossing. It had subsequently throughout the Aisne fighting been forced to occupy trenches in the low ground by the river, which were throughout dominated by the German artillery on the heights beyond. Then, within one week of leaving the Aisne trenches, they were once more engaged in ceaseless battling day and night against superior numbers, for on the several battalions of this division in turn devolved the paramount duty of holding the Givenchy position at all costs.

That night Sir Horace motored twenty-five miles over to St. Omer to explain the situation to the C. in C., who was most sympathetic and promised that he would send all that he could spare of the Lahore Indians to be at Estaires at eight o'clock next morning, with a rider to the effect that they were not to be used except in emergency, as they were destined for other work. As a matter of fact they were not used, the 5th Division proving equal to the occasion without foreign assistance.

Throughout the 23rd, 24th and 25th the Germans continued to attack Givenchy with the utmost persistence, but without succeeding in dislodging the Devons. That gallant regiment, however, was becoming very weak in officers. During their three days at Canteleux, Captain Chichester and Lieutenant Ridgers had been killed, and Colonel Gloster and Lieutenant Tillett wounded. Then on the 24th, Lieutenant Ainslie was killed, and on the following day Captain Besley and Lieutenant Quick were killed, the latter while running to the next regiment to tell them that the Devons meant holding on and that they must do the same. On the 20th they relieved the Manchesters at Festubert. The latter regiment, during its occupation of Festubert, had held its difficult position with magnificent determination and had won two Victoria Crosses, 2nd Lieutenant Leach and Sergeant Hogan being each awarded the Cross for valour.

On the following day, the whole line in the neighbourhood of Festubert was subjected to a particularly infernal shelling, every known species of missile being hurled against it. The Devons stood firm through it all, but the regiment on their left—an Indian regiment for the first time in the firing line—found it too much for them, and after having lost most of their officers they retired, their trenches being at once occupied by the enemy. This made the position of the Devons very precarious. With as little delay as possible the reserve company of the regiment under Lieutenant Hancock and Lieutenant Dunsterville was brought up, and with great gallantry the company attacked and drove the Germans out of the right-hand section of the lost trenches, the 58th Vaughan Rifles at the same time retaking the left-hand section. Both Lieutenant Hancock and Lieutenant Dunsterville were killed during the charge, and Lieutenant Ditmas thereupon took over command of the company, but he himself was subsequently killed, after displaying conspicuous gallantry. On the 31st, as a part of the general process of transfer, the Devons were at length relieved, after sixteen days of almost continuous fighting. They received a great ovation from the other troops on their withdrawal. Lieutenant-Colonel Gloster was given the C.M.G. and Lieutenant Worrall the Military Cross. Other officers who showed conspicuous ability and daring were Lieutenants Lang, Prior and Alexander. Sergeant-Major Webb, who on several occasions had given proof of remarkable courage and coolness, got the D.C.M., as also did Lance-Corporal Simmons and Private Worsfold, the latter of whom greatly distinguished himself by carrying numerous messages at Festubert after the telegraphic communication was cut.

We have now, however, got considerably ahead of the general situation, from which we digressed on October 22nd in order to keep in touch with the position at and around Givenchy. We must therefore once more take up the thread at that date.

During the 23rd, 24th and 25th there was no movement of marked importance in the southern area, but continuous attacks all along the line still further reduced the number and vitality of the 5th Division, and by the evening of the 25th it was rapidly becoming evident to all concerned that the condition of that division, and indeed of the entire 2nd A.C. in greater or less degree, was extremely serious. The casualties of this army corps since its arrival in Flanders now amounted to 350 officers and 8,204 men, and those that survived were in a state of extreme exhaustion both mental and physical.

Sir Horace summoned General Maude, Colonel Martyn (who had taken over the command of the 13th Brigade when Colonel Hickie had been invalided home on October 13th), and Count Gleichen, the three brigadiers of the 5th Division, to meet General Morland, and all agreed that the situation was very grave indeed, and that human endurance was nearly at the breaking point. General Maude (14th Brigade), however, reported that Colonel Ballard was determined to hold the canal trenches with the Norfolks to the last gasp, and that the Devons next the Norfolks at Givenchy were equally resolute, though terribly thinned by casualties. All, however, agreed that however willing the spirit might be, the flesh was too weak to make any prolonged resistance. The Generals themselves were well-nigh worn out with the ceaseless strain, and with want of sleep, their nights being largely occupied in motoring hither and thither for purposes of consultation with other commanders. Two or three hours' sleep in a night was a luxury. Luckily the Germans—accurate as their information usually was—seem to have failed to realize the extreme exhaustion of the troops facing them at this part of the line, otherwise the history of events might have been different.

CHAPTER 21

Neuve Chapelle

The 3rd Division had perhaps, if anything, been so far less highly tried in the way of ceaseless fighting against odds than the 5th Division, but any deficiency in this respect was fully made up to them by the fighting at Neuve Chapelle on the 25th, 26th and 27th.

This very costly three days' fighting opened on the night of the 25th, during a heavy downpour of rain which succeeded a beautiful day, by a furious attack, from the neighbourhood of the Bois de Biez, on the left of the 7th Brigade and the right of the 8th Brigade. This wood, which played a prominent part in these three days' fighting, lies about half a mile to the south-east of Neuve Chapelle, in the centre of the equilateral triangle formed by that place, Aubers and Illies. The Germans advanced out of the wood with great courage and with every appearance of meaning business, but the 7th Brigade and the 15th Sikhs, who had taken over from Conneau's cavalry the day before, managed to stand their ground, and in the end drove the enemy back with very heavy loss, though themselves suffering severely, the Sikhs, who fought superbly, alone losing 200 in officers and men.

The 8th Brigade was not so fortunate, the R. Irish Rifles, who were the right-hand battalion, being driven out of their trenches, which lay north of the La Bassée road on the east side of the village. The situation for the moment was critical, but the lost trenches were very gallantly retaken by the 4th Middlesex, led by Colonel Hull, and the 4th R. Fusiliers. The latter battalion suffered considerably in the operation, Lieutenants Hope-Johnstone and Waller being killed. This battalion had now only 200 men left. The whole of the 9th Brigade, in fact, had been reduced to mere skeletons. This brigade (Shaw's) had a magnificent record behind it.[1] From the time when, at Mons, it had borne the brunt of the German attack and put up such a magnificent defence, it had never failed in any task for which it had been called upon; and it is possible that its great fighting reputation and the cheerfulness with which it undertook any duty assigned it, coupled with the undoubted military talents of its Brigadier, had earned for it rather more than its fair share of difficult and dangerous work. During the past fortnight it had fought with great gallantry and with invariable success, and during that short period it had lost 54 officers and 1,400 men.

On the following day the attack was renewed, the Germans suddenly swarming once again out of the Bois de Biez opposite, and the R. Irish Rifles were again driven in, their trenches being at once occupied by the enemy, many of whom entered the town and remained there throughout the day.

The 7th Brigade on the right and the 9th Brigade on the left now had the Germans wedged in between them. The Northumberland Fusiliers (the old Fighting Fifth) on the right of the 9th Brigade, now found the position untenable in the weak numerical condition to which they had been reduced, and they were compelled to withdraw to the western side of the town. During this withdrawal, which was carried out in excellent order, Corporal Fisk found time to extinguish some flames which were enveloping the limber of one of our guns—a gallant act performed under very heavy fire for which he was given the D.C.M.

On the night of the 26th the position at Neuve Chapelle was a curious one. The enemy were in possession of all the trenches on the north-east side of the town, but on the south-east side the Wiltshire Regiment, the R. West Kents, the K.O.Y.L.I. and the East Surrey were still holding their ground, in advance of the town. The rest of the 3rd Division were thrown back behind the town.

About 11 a.m. on the 27th the usual morning attack was made on the Wiltshire Regiment, whose left flank was now, of course, quite unprotected, and by noon they too had been forced to retire, the Germans in great numbers following closely on their heels. The

---

1. 4th R. Fusiliers, 1st R. Scots Fusiliers, Northumberland Fusiliers and the Lincolnshire Regiment.

position of the R. West Kents was now most precarious, as they had the enemy on three sides of them, and it seemed inevitable that they must follow the example of the several regiments on their left, who had been successively forced to give way. Such, however, was not their opinion, and, undismayed by the apparent hopelessness of their position, they promptly set about preparing a defence which proved to be one of the most remarkable of the campaign. Major Buckle, who was in command, on seeing the Wiltshires forced back, at once made his way to the left of his battalion in order to reorganize the formation so as to meet the altered conditions, but he was almost immediately killed, Captain Legard being killed at the same time and Lieutenants Williams and Holloway wounded. All the company officers on the left flank were now down, but the new movement was carried out under the direction of Sergeant-Major Penny and Sergeant-Major Crossley, the reserve company wheeling to its left, while the left of the firing line threw back its flank, so as to present a convex face to the position now occupied by the enemy. All this was carried out under a murderous fire. In this formation the battalion held on till the evening, when our troops in rear of the town counter-attacked with momentary success. This success was mainly brought about by the 47th Sikhs and the 9th Bhopal Regiment, who made a fine dash into the town from the direction of Croix Barbée, the first-named regiment showing great courage, but they both suffered heavy losses from the ubiquitous German machine-guns in the houses. At the same time three groups of the French Cyclist Corps made an attack from the Pont Logis side. The impetus of these combined attacks drove the Germans back for the time being, and indeed for the whole of that night, but their concealed machine-guns continued to play havoc in the ranks of the assailants, and in the early morning of the 28th the attacking force had to fall back, the Germans once more re-occupying the town.

The position of the R. West Kents was now as bad again as ever, and once more half the battalion had to face about to its left flank and rear. The execution of this movement again took its toll of officers, Captain Battersby and Lieutenant Gore being killed, and Lieutenant Moulton-Barratt wounded. The battalion had now lost twelve out of the fourteen officers with which it had gone into these trenches, 2nd Lieutenant White and 2nd Lieutenant Russell alone being left, and on these two it now devolved to maintain the spirit of the corps. The remarkable position had by this time developed that practically the whole of Neuve Chapelle was in the hands of the enemy, with the exception of the little south-east corner by the La Bassée road, which was still stubbornly held by the undefeated R. West Kents. On the other side of the La Bassée road, and in the angle which that road makes with the Richebourg road, the K.O.Y.L.I. were still standing firm with the East Surrey beyond them, but these last two regiments were not so hardly pressed, the main attack being always on the eastern side of the main La Bassée road.

We must now take a glance at the Neuve Chapelle position from the larger military point of view. The counter-attacks on the 27th had failed mainly owing to the exhaustion and insufficiency of the troops employed. The place, however, being of considerable strategic importance (to us), the Divisional headquarters determined that it could not be left in the hands of the enemy, and an attack on a more important scale was therefore organized for the following day. Sir Horace motored across at night and saw General Conneau, who told him that in addition to the six hundred Chasseurs already in the line, he could lend him a regiment of dismounted cavalry and nine batteries of artillery. The C. in C. also sent him the 2nd C.B. under Colonel Mullens, of which the 4th Dragoon Guards arrived on the evening of the 27th, the 9th Lancers and 18th Hussars during the early part of the night. The whole were placed under the command of General McCracken of the 7th Brigade, to whom the details of the attack on the following day were entrusted.

At 8 a.m. on the 28th, some two hours after the Indians and French cyclists had been forced to retire, proceedings were started with a general bombardment of the village. This was a matter of some little delicacy on account of the position still held by the R. West Kents and K.O.Y.L.I., and the difficulty was not made lighter by the fog which lay thick on the plain in the early hours of the morning. In the circumstances the accuracy of the French artillery was remarkable. The north side of the village was given a great bombardment, and at eleven o'clock the sun came through, the fog cleared, and the infantry attack began. The artillery had now played its part, but, to assist in the assault, one gun of the 41st Battery was pushed forward to the junction of the Armentières and La Bassée roads. From this point of vantage it was able to work considerable execution on the German infantry massed in the north-east corner of the village, but, as an inevitable consequence, was itself singled out for special attention on the part of the enemy. At the same time, as the attack became more general, its sphere of usefulness became greatly circumscribed, and finally Lieutenant Lowell, who was in command, resolved to make an attempt to report the position to his C.O. with a view to getting further instructions. To do this, however, it was necessary to leave his shelter and negotiate a hundred yards of bullet-swept road. He was hit almost at once, but kept on his way till a second bullet brought him down in the road. A gunner of the name of Spicer thereupon ran out to get him under cover, but was himself at once knocked over, and subsequently died. Bomb. Bloomfield then went out to the assistance of his officer and comrade, and was fortunate enough to get them both under cover without himself being wounded.

In the meanwhile, the infantry attack was gallantly pressed home, the 47th Sikhs and the 2nd C.B. (on foot) fighting splendidly from street to street. In spite of all, however, the attack once more failed, and at 5 p.m. the Germans were still in possession of the village, always excepting the one small corner still held by the R. West Kents and K.O.Y.L.I.

The anticlimax of the whole thing, and a cause for reflection as to the objects for which modern armies fight one another, is furnished by the fact that in the evening the Germans quietly vacated the town, apparently realizing—after the sacrifice of some 5,000 men—that the position was either untenable, or was not worth the cost of keeping. Our losses in the last day's fighting alone amounted to 65 officers and 1,466 men. The heroes of the three days' fighting were of course the R. West Kents, who immortalized themselves by a performance which in many ways must be unique. The two surviving officers, 2nd Lieutenants White and Russell, were each awarded the D.S.O., and were, in addition, the subjects of some particularly flattering remarks on the part of Sir Horace. The two Sergeant-Majors above referred to were each given the D.C.M., as also was Sergeant Stroud and Private Alison. At 2 a.m. on the 29th, the battalion was finally relieved by the Seaforths, having lost over 300 men in the Neuve Chapelle trenches.

This affair of Neuve Chapelle marks the close of the 2nd A.C. operations in the La Bassée district. On the 31st the British troops began to be formally relieved by General Willcocks and his Indians. This corps had now been augmented by the arrival of the Ferozapore Brigade, to be followed almost immediately by the Secunderabad Cavalry Brigade and the Jodhpur Lancers. By 10 a.m. on the 31st the transfer of positions was complete, and Sir Horace and his gallant but war-worn A.C. withdrew to Hazebrouck. A certain proportion of the 2nd A.C. was afterwards called upon to support General Willcocks, but for the most part we shall, in the future, find them co-operating with the 1st A.C. and the 7th Division in the neighbourhood of Ypres.

As far, then, as this record of events goes, we may now bid farewell to the fighting area between Armentières and La Bassée, and follow exclusively the events east and south of Ypres. These were destined to develop into a succession of battles, in which small numbers of British troops successfully opposed large numbers of German troops, and the details of which furnish, in the words of Sir J. French, "one of the most glorious chapters in the annals of the British army."

CHAPTER 22

Pilkem

Having now taken a permanent farewell of the fighting in the La Bassée area, with a view to following uninterruptedly the more exciting situation which had gradually been developing around Ypres it becomes necessary once more to pick up the thread of the northern doings where it was dropped.

It will be remembered that on Oct. 19th, 20th and 21st there had been very fierce fighting in and around Zonnebeke, where the enemy made persistent efforts to break through to Ypres—efforts which were frustrated by the timely arrival of the 1st A.C. on the night of the 20th, This Army Corps during the night took over the entire line from Bixschoote to Zonnebeke, and on the 21st the Guards' Brigade, on the right of this line, was able to contribute largely to the repulse of the German attack.

On the 22nd the pressure was shifted to the left of the 1st A.C. line, the 1st Brigade being attacked in great force at Pilkem from the direction of Staden. The Germans advanced to their attack with the utmost determination and with a complete disregard of danger, singing *Die wacht am Rhein* and waving their rifles over their heads. The focus-point of the attack was the position occupied by the Camerons, who eventually, by sheer weight of numbers, were driven back, but not before they had taken an appalling toll of the enemy, 1,500 of the latter being found dead upon the ground the following day.

General Lomax, commanding the division, had no idea of leaving the enemy in peace to enjoy this temporary triumph, and at nine o'clock on the same evening the 2nd Brigade, which was billeted some eight or nine miles to the south at the village of Boes-inghe, received orders to retake the lost trenches. The R. Sussex regiment was left at Boesinghe, but the remaining three battalions, *viz.*, the 1st Loyal N. Lancashires, the 2nd K.R.R. (60th) and the 1st Northamptons, set out and marched all night to the little village of Pilkem, which was reached at 5 a.m.

The brigade, which had had no food all night, was given no time for rest or breakfast, but was ordered to attack the trenches at once. In the brigade order of October 28th, dealing with this action, General Bulfin, the Brigadier, singles out the 1st Loyal N. Lancashire Regiment for special praise. It may, therefore, be al-lowable to confine our description of the action to a brief review of the part played by this battalion, which, it will be remem-bered, had behaved with such remarkable gallantry at the battle of Troyon.

At 6 o'clock, in the dim light of an autumn morning, the bri-gade set out from Pilkem. The lost trenches lay more or less par-allel to the Bixschoote to Langemarck road, a mile to the north of Pilkem. The attacking troops advanced in line, the K.R.R. being on the left, the Loyal N. Lancashires in the centre, with the Northamptons on the right. The 2nd S. Staffords and the 1st Queen's (from the 3rd Brigade) were in support. In this order they advanced to within 300 yards of the trenches, where they began to come under a very heavy rifle fire. Major Carter,[1] com-manding the L. N. Lancashires, decided to charge at once with the bayonet, and he sent a message to this effect to the K.R.R. on his left, asking them to advance with him. This, however, they were unable to do, and Major Carter accordingly decided to at-tack alone. Captain Henderson, with the machine-gun section, pushed forward to a very advanced position on the left, from which he was able to get a clear field for his guns, and the bat-talion formed up for the attack. Captain Crane's and Captain Prince's companies were in the first line; the other two were in support. The order to fix bayonets was given; a bugler sounded the "Charge," and with loud cheers the battalion dashed forward,

---

1. Major Carter, D.S.O., was killed on November 10th, 1914. He was the third O.C. the Loyal N. Lancs, to be killed in action, Colonel Lloyd having fallen on September 14th and Colonel Knight at the battle of the Marne.

and in less than ten minutes had carried the trenches and cleared them of the enemy. Six hundred prisoners were taken, a number which might have been increased but that further pursuit was checked by our own artillery.

During this most gallant charge on the part of the Loyal N. Lancashires, the Queen's and Northamptons on the right advanced and occupied the inn at the cross-roads, where the road from Pilkem joins the main road to Langemarck.

The victory was now complete. The L. N. Lancashires lost 6 officers and 150 men killed and wounded. They won, however, very high praise from the brigadier and from General Lomax, the divisional general. Captain Henderson was awarded the Military Cross for. . .

. . . conspicuous gallantry and ability on Oct. 23rd, when, with his machine-gun detachment, he performed most valuable services in the final attack and charge, inflicting heavy losses on the enemy. He pushed his guns close up to a flank, and helped in a great degree to clear the enemy's trenches.

One cannot convey a sense of the really remarkable nature of this performance better than by quoting the words of General Bulfin in the G.O. already referred to. It says:

In spite of the stubborn resistance offered by the German troops, the object of the engagement was accomplished, but not without many casualties in the brigade. By nightfall the trenches previously captured by the Germans had been re-occupied, about 600 prisoners captured, and fully 1,500 German dead were lying out in front of our trenches. The Brigadier-General congratulates the L. N. Lancashires, the Northamptons and the K.R.R. but desires especially to commend the fine soldierlike spirit of the L. N. Lancashires, which advancing steadily under heavy shell and rifle fire, and aided by its machine-guns, were enabled to form up within a comparatively short distance of the enemy's trenches. Fixing bayonets, the battalion then charged, carried the trenches, and then occupied them, and to them must be allotted the majority of the prisoners captured.

The Brigadier-General congratulates himself on having in his brigade a battalion which, after marching the whole of the previous night, without food or rest, was able to maintain its splendid record in the past by the determination and self-sacrifice displayed in this action.

CHAPTER 23

The Second Advance

The 2nd Brigade remained in the position it had captured for twenty-four hours, when it was relieved by the French. In fact during the night of the 23rd and the morning of the 24th the entire line from Bixschoote to Zonnebeke, which the 1st A.C. had taken over from the 3rd Cavalry Division three days earlier, was in turn taken over from them by the French, a Division of the 87th Territorials relieving the 1st Division between Bixschoote and Langemarck, and the 18th Corps of the 9th French Army taking the place of the 2nd Division from Langemarck to Zonnebeke.

The 1st Division went into reserve at Ypres, whilst the 2nd Division moved down to its right across the Zonnebeke road, and took over the position of the 22nd Brigade, which also went back into reserve with its numbers sadly thinned by the fighting of the last three days.

On the following night the 1st Division came up on the right of the 2nd Division and took over the line from west of Reutel to the Menin road, thus relieving the 7th Division of any further responsibility north of that road.

This proved to be the final shuffle of the Ypres defence force, and the positions now taken over proved—broadly speaking—to be permanent. It will be well, therefore, for a thorough understanding of what followed, that these positions should be clearly fixed in the reader's mind. They were as follows: North of the Zonnebeke road the French had now taken over entire charge. From the Zonnebeke road to a point near the race-course in the Polygon wood, west of Reutel, was the 2nd Division; on its right, reaching to the

Menin road, was the 1st Division, and from the Menin road to Zandvoorde the 7th Division, with the 3rd Cavalry Division in the Zandvoorde trenches. So far, so good. Our line was everywhere strengthened and consolidated. Between Zonnebeke and Zandvoorde three divisions now occupied the ground hitherto held by the three brigades of the 7th Division; but, on the other hand, fresh German troops were daily arriving in their thousands at Roulers and Menin, and though the line of our resistance might be stronger, the pressure of attack was correspondingly increased.

The shortening and thickening of our line was not, as events proved, accomplished one moment too soon, for on the morning of the 24th the British position was attacked all along its length with a determination which could hardly have been withstood by the attenuated line of a week before.

The 2nd Battalion of the Warwickshire Regiment accomplished a fine achievement on this morning. At dawn they were marched away from Zonnebeke to retake the trenches south of Reutel out of which the Wiltshire Regiment had been shelled. The operation entailed an advance of a mile over ground which was constantly under fire. The final act was the rushing of the German position, the nucleus of which was a small detached farm-house in which were several machine-guns. Colonel Loring, who had already been wounded, himself led this last charge and fell dead in the act. The house, however, was captured and the whole German position rushed and occupied, the enemy being driven out with very considerable loss. The Warwicks lost 105 men and several officers.

Almost at the same moment a very similar act, in many respects, was performed by Captain Dunlop's company of the 1st S. Staffords, which it will be remembered had been detached from its battalion on the 21st for the support of the Northumberland Hussars. Here again a farm-house bristling with machine-guns had to be rushed, and here again in the very moment of victory the leader fell dead.

These single company engagements were a special characteristic of the fighting at this period. Owing to our scarcity of men, it was seldom that an entire battalion could be spared for purposes of support, and single companies were consequently sent hither and thither to do the work of battalions—to fill gaps, strengthen weak spots, and even—as sometimes happened—to retake lost positions and drive back parties of the enemy which had broken through. A case in point on this very morning of October 24th was that of No. 4 Company 1st Grenadier Guards. The circumstances here were that the Germans had succeeded in breaking through the right flank of the 21st Brigade, and, as serious consequences threatened, a counter-attack was ordered to be made by Major Colby with No. 4 Company of the Grenadiers, who were at the time on the left of the 20th Brigade. The undertaking in this case was an extremely difficult and dangerous one, both on account of the numerical insufficiency of a single company for the task assigned it, and also because the attack entailed the negotiation of our own barbed wire entanglement. This entanglement, it need scarcely be said, was under a very constant fire from the enemy, making the undertaking, on the face of it, almost a hopeless one. However, it was done. The Grenadiers crawled through, over or under the wire, reformed on the far side, charged and drove the enemy back once more to their own lines. The losses of the Grenadiers were very severe, and, as in the case of the other two companies, the leader, Major Colby, fell dead at the head of his men. Lieutenant Antrobus was also killed and Captain Leatham was severely wounded. In the meanwhile the 5th Brigade had been brought up from reserve and completed the rout of the enemy.

On the same morning the 6th Brigade, which had taken over the position of the 22nd Brigade south of the Zonnebeke road, began pushing forward with the ambitious view of re-occupying the advance trenches originally held by the 7th Division along the Paschendael—Becelaere road. The 1st Berkshire Regiment, under Colonel Graham, was on the left of the brigade next the road, with the King's Regiment on its right, the other two battalions being in support. In this formation the brigade now advanced with such dash and vigour as completely to outstrip the troops to right and left. The woods in front were full of Germans; every yard gained had to be fought for, and there were considerable casualties, Colonel Bannatyne, of the King's, being amongst those killed. However, the brigade made its point and got into the old trenches, but as the French on the north side of the road had not succeeded in making the same progress, the position was a precarious one, and two companies of the Berkshire Regiment had to be thrown back almost at right angles, that is to say, parallel with the road, in order to cover the half mile which separated them. The performance of this regiment was a distinctly meritorious one, several guns being captured as well as prisoners, and it was duly recognized as such in high quarters, Lieutenant Nicholson and Lieutenant Hanbury-Sparrow getting the D.S.O. for their conduct on this occasion, while Sergeant-Major Smith, Sergeant Taylor and Private Bossom were awarded the D.C.M.

The push and enterprise of this regiment on the 24th roused the activity and emulation of the whole division, which, on the following morning, was ordered to advance against Reutel. The attack opened with a furious bombardment of that place by our artillery, and in the afternoon the 4th Brigade was ordered to clear the Polygon wood, the object now being to bring up the 4th and 5th Brigades in line with the 6th.

The 4th Brigade advanced with the Irish Guards and 2nd Grenadiers in the front line, the two Coldstream battalions being in support. Night fell before any great advance could be made. The night was one of torrential rain, which the troops passed in the extremity of misery waiting for the dawn. The attack was then resumed, the 2nd Coldstream coming up into line between the Irish Guards and the Grenadiers. Later on the 3rd Coldstream were also brought up into line on the right of the Grenadiers. The 5th Brigade was on the right of the 4th. Good progress was made, and the line with the 6th Brigade having been established, the men dug themselves in at dusk. This wearisome but highly necessary step had hardly been completed before a furious counter-attack was made at 10 p.m. It was, however, repulsed with loss, and the 2nd Division, cold, wet and weary, remained unmolested for the rest of the night.

This successful advance on the 26th was—as far as this chronicle is concerned—the last act of the 4th (Guards) Brigade as an integral unit. From this time on, the 2nd Grenadiers and the Irish Guards will be found acting quite independently in another part of the field, under the command of Lord Cavan, while the 2nd and 3rd Coldstream remained in the Polygon wood trenches under Colonel Pereira. Later on these two Coldstream battalions were joined by the remnant of the 1st Battalion from the 1st Brigade, so that the regiment was, in fact, consolidated. It is important in view of subsequent events to keep this clearly in mind. The Coldstream—with the exception of the 1st Battalion—will not again appear in these pages as actors in the great Ypres drama. But though not directly under the limelight, the role allotted to them henceforth was probably as trying as that to which any regiment could be subjected. For twenty-two consecutive days from the date of the advance they occupied the Polygon wood trenches. In the case of the 3rd Battalion these trenches zigzagged along the eastern edge of the wood, while the 2nd Battalion trenches ran through the wood itself and were straight. In each case the general lie was north and south, in contrast to the trenches of the 6th Brigade on their left, which faced north-east, making, in fact, the first bend back in the Ypres salient. These Polygon wood trenches proved most abominably wet even for Flanders, the neighbourhood abounding in springs which kept them half full of water even in dry weather. Here the Coldstreamers stayed unrelieved for over three weeks, up to their knees in water, under ceaseless shell-fire, and sniped at with horrible precision on every occasion when they raised their heads. To add to the unpleasantness of the position, the woods in front were thick with unburied Germans, from which the whole atmosphere was polluted. Luckily during the whole of their tenure the wind blew from westerly quarters, which while it brought abominably wet weather, nevertheless blew the tainted air in the direction of the enemy.

CHAPTER 24

The Fighting at Kruiseik

While four of the Guards' battalions were thus pushing their way through the Polygon wood near Reutel, the two Guards' battalions in the 20th Brigade were enacting a small drama of their own at the village of Kruiseik, south of the Menin road. Here two companies of the Scots Guards, and the King's Company, 1st Grenadiers, had been posted in some advance trenches east of the village in the direction of the country road running from the village of Vieux Chien to Werwick. About 8.30 at night these advance trenches were attempted by peculiarly German methods. Through the intense darkness that reigned that night, and through the torrential rain, the enemy crept up close to our lines with the aid of every device known to twentieth century warfare. Some said they had come to surrender, others said they were the S. Staffords, and others again called appealingly for Captain Paynter, who was, in actual fact, in command of the right-hand of the two Scots Guards companies. That officer's response, however, took the form of a well-directed fire, and the friendly inquirers departed with some haste. Lord Claud Hamilton (1st Grenadiers), who was in charge of the machine-gun section, was also undeceived by the friendliness of the visitors, and his maxims contributed to the haste of their departure. This officer had now been seven days and nights, unrelieved, in the machine-gun trenches, and the coolness and resource which he displayed during that period gained for him the D.S.O. He was relieved early on the morning following this night attack by an officer of the Scots Guards, who was killed the same day.

The inhospitable reception of the enemy above described

made the night attack a distinct failure as far as Captain Paynter's company was concerned. The left-hand trenches were less fortunate. It may be that they were more unsuspecting, or perhaps the British accent of the figures advancing through the darkness was purer on the left than on the right. In any event a report reached the battalion headquarters in rear about nine o'clock that these trenches had been rushed and all the occupants killed. On receipt of this news the two reserve companies of the Scots Guards were sent up under Major the Hon. H. Fraser to investigate, and if necessary to retake the lost trenches. These two companies filed silently through the main street of Kruiseik, keeping close under the shadow of the houses on either side. Not a light was burning, and not a sound was to be heard.

At the far end of the village Major Fraser halted the column, and went forward alone to try and get in touch with Captain Paynter in the right-hand forward trenches, and find out from him what the truth of the matter really was. He managed after a time to find that officer, who assured him that not only were his own trenches still uncaptured, but that he had every intention of keeping them so. As to the trenches on his left he knew nothing. With this information Major Fraser made his way back to the east end of the village, where he had left his men. He decided to investigate for himself the truth as to the left-hand trenches, and, accordingly, accompanied by Lieutenant Holbeche, in the capacity of guide, and forty men, he crept down the cinder track which led from the road to the trenches in question. The trenches were in absolute silence, and he was beginning to doubt the story of their occupation, when suddenly a flashlight was turned on to his party, a word of command rang out, and a volley broke the stillness of the night. Major Fraser gave the word to charge, and the little party dashed forward with fixed bayonets, but they were shot down before the trenches were reached. Major Fraser was killed and Lieutenant Holbeche severely wounded, and of the whole party only four returned.

In the meanwhile the rest of the two companies which had been waiting at the end of the village street noticed a light in a house standing by itself in the fields. Lord Dalrymple and Captain Fox held a consultation and decided to surround it. When this was done, Sergeant Mitchell, with great courage, went up to the door and knocked. It was flung open and he was at once shot dead. The house, however, was well surrounded, and all within it were taken prisoners. They numbered over two hundred, including seven officers, and they were promptly sent to the rear under escort. Further back, however, the prisoners were transferred to the custody of some of the 2nd Queen's, and the Scots Guards escort rejoined the two companies at the end of the village, whereupon the lost trenches were attacked and re-captured, and connection once more established with Captain Paynter.[1] This was not effected without considerable further loss. In addition to those already mentioned, Lieutenants Gladwin and Dormer were killed, and Colonel Bolton, Lord Dalrymple, Captain Fox, Lord G. Grosvenor, and the Hon. J. Coke were all wounded, and, in the darkness of the night, fell into the enemy's hands. The 2nd Scots Guards in all lost nine officers during this night's fighting. On the following day the battalion was ordered to abandon the Kruiseik trenches, and was taken back into reserve, mustering only 450.

The withdrawal of the 2nd Scots Guards from the trenches east of Kruiseik, which it had cost them so dearly to hold, marks the first step in our retirement from the advanced position we had taken up, following the forward movement of October 19th, and consequently the first step in the straightening out of the salient bulge. They were not replaced, and this ground passed permanently out of our hands.

The King's Company, 1st Grenadiers, which, it will be remembered, were also posted in the advance trenches east of Kruiseik, by some means failed to receive the order to withdraw, with the result that, on the afternoon of the 26th, they found themselves absolutely isolated, and cut off from their army by the better part of half a mile. The position, on the face of it, appeared absolutely hopeless, as the Germans were by this time in occupation of the village of Kruiseik itself. However, as the Guards, like the Samurai, do not surrender while yet unwounded, they faced the situation, and actually fought their way back through the main street of the village. The Germans had machine-guns in the windows of the houses, but for once in a way these weapons were less effective than usual, and in the evening the company rejoined its battalion, considerably

1. Captain Paynter and Captain Fox got the D.S.O. for their share in the night's work.

thinned in numbers, but triumphant. Lieutenant Somerset was the only officer killed during this retirement.

The night of the 25th was a bad one in every way for the 20th Brigade, and the wastage of life owing to the darkness, and the rain, and the impossibility of distinguishing friend from foe, is not good to think upon. Here is another instance.

The 1st S. Staffords were attached for the moment to the 20th Brigade, to which brigade they were acting reserve. Before the Scots Guards had recovered the lost trenches, that is to say, while these and the buildings in rear of them were still in the occupation of the enemy, Captain Ransford was ordered up with a platoon of the S. Staffords to reinforce the firing line. In carrying out this order he came under fire both from the Germans in front and from our own troops in rear, and the whole detachment was practically wiped out. Captain Ransford himself, with great courage, went forward alone through the impenetrable darkness to try and sift the position, and discover who was who, but he fell in the attempt and was seen no more. There is consolation in the probability that losses owing to mistaken identity were not confined to our side.

The 1st S. Staffords during the confused and sanguinary fighting of these two days, that is to say, the 25th and 26th, lost 13 officers and 440 rank and file. As has so often happened in this war, the battalion in reserve was called upon for much of the most strenuous work, and in this particular case the S. Staffords had at one time or another to support each of the four units of the 20th Brigade. Much of this work was of a particularly difficult and dangerous nature, and in the darkness and confusion that prevailed the various units were apt at times to get very greatly mixed up, and to lapse into the condition of sheep without any accredited shepherd.

At one very critical moment in the ebb and flow of battle, it happened that the C.O., Colonel Ovens, who was at the time in an advanced position with two companies of the S. Staffords, noticed a mob of some 300 men of these mixed units retiring on his left. He sent off Captain White, the Quarter-Master of the regiment, to find out the cause. The reply was that an order had been received to retire. Captain White—suspecting German methods, or, at any rate, suspecting that the order originated with someone who was interested in its fulfilment—by super-human efforts succeeded in rallying the men and leading them back into the firing line, an act which beyond any question had a marked effect on the fortunes of the day, or, rather, of the night.

The desperate fighting of this period at and around Kruiseik will always be associated with the 20th Brigade. The other two brigades in the 7th Division were shifted about, as occasion required, to various points between Zonnebeke and Zandvoorde; but from October 19th to the 29th, the 20th Brigade operated at Kruiseik alone. The gradual annihilation of this splendid brigade—possibly the finest in the whole army—forms a story which is no less stirring than it is tragic. The tragedy is obvious, but it is relieved by the thought of the superb devotion of each of the battalions that formed the command of General Ruggles-Brise. Each battalion, in its own allotted sphere, fought to a finish. Each battalion in its turn furnished an example of unflinching heroism which is an epic in itself. They not only fought till there were no more left to fight, but they fought up to the very end with success. It must have been a consolation to their gallant brigadier, when in the end he was carried off the field with a shattered thigh, to feel that he had survived long enough to share in a glory which will never be excelled.

The worst sufferer in the early days of the Kruiseik fighting was the 2nd Battalion of the Border Regiment. The experiences of this regiment are of the highest interest, as being typical of the hold-on-at-all-costs spirit which animated the British force during the period of the German advance, and which was responsible for the miscarriage of all the desperate efforts of the enemy to break through. On October 22nd the battalion was posted along the road from Zandvoorde, at the point where it cuts the Kruiseik—Werwick road. Their trenches formed an ugly salient, which was commanded on three sides by the enemy's artillery, and at which particularly accurate practice could be, and was, made by the German batteries posted on the America ridge, about a mile to the south-east. Their instructions were to hold on to these trenches *at all costs* till relieved. They did hold on, and on the 27th they were relieved—at least, those of them that were left.

146

Their relaxation during those six days consisted in counting the shells directed at them, and speculating as to the accuracy of the next shot. The constant prayer of every officer and man was for an infantry attack of some sort—German or British. The prayer was not answered. Their orders were to hold on at all costs till relieved. They were not relieved, so they held on. On the 24th, 25th and 26th the shells fell in or around their trenches at the rate of two per minute from dawn till dark. Their casualties from this shell-fire averaged 150 a day and the enemy's guns fired unchallenged and unmolested by our own artillery. In those days the numerical superiority of the German artillery was overwhelming, and, as an inevitable consequence, our infantry afforded them passive but diminishing targets. In the case of the Border Regiment the target diminished rapidly. On the 23rd Captain Gordon and 2nd Lieutenant Clancy were killed; on the 25th Major Allen and Lieutenant Warren were killed, and Lieutenant Clegg wounded; on the 26th Captain Lees, Captain Cholmondeley, Captain Andrews and Lieutenant Surtees were killed, and Major Bosanquet and Lieutenant Bevis were wounded. On the 27th the 300 men that remained were relieved—for the moment.

On the afternoon of the 26th the pressure against this battalion became so severe, and their casualties were so high, that at two o'clock General Kavanagh was ordered to make a demonstration with the 7th C.B. in the direction of Zandvoorde, with a view to diverting some of the pressure. The 1st Life Guards were already in occupation of the Zandvoorde trenches, and the demonstration was entrusted to the Blues, who were, at the time, the reserve regiment to the brigade. The Blues were at Klein Zillebeke when the order arrived, and they at once got mounted and galloped along the road that connects that place with Zandvoorde. Lord Alastair Ker's squadron, which was leading, rode right through the 1st Life Guards trenches, and, turning to the right at the top of the ridge, dismounted and opened fire. Their squadron immediately came under a heavy fire and its casualties were considerable. In the meanwhile the other two squadrons of the Blues (Captain Brassey's and Captain Harrison's), dismounted behind the Life Guards, and advanced to the top of the ridge on foot, supporting the fire of the leading squadron. The demonstration was kept up till darkness fell, when the regiment, having carried out its orders with complete success, retired to a château between Klein Zillebeke and Hollebeke, where it billeted for the night. Lord Alastair Ker and Trooper Nevin were both decorated for their gallantry on this occasion.

The continuation of the Zandvoorde trenches further south was still in the occupation of the 10th Hussars. These were heavily shelled all through the day, and the casualties among their officers continued to be on a high scale, Sir F. Rose and Lieutenant Turnor being killed, and Major Crichton wounded.

CHAPTER 25

The Last of Kruiseik

The next two days were days of comparative calm—the lull before the desperate storm which was preparing to break upon the British force. On the morning of the 27th, the 6th Brigade, on the left of our line, which had so successfully pushed forward its position on the 24th, made a still further advance, the 1st K.R.R. on this occasion being the left-hand battalion, with the 1st S. Staffords on its right. The 1st Berks and the King's Regiment were in support. The movement was again a complete success, the brigade advancing as far as the Paschendael—Becelaere road and occupying the crest of the ridge along which this road runs. Here the K.R.R. came under a very heavy shell-fire, and Prince Maurice of Battenberg and Captain Wells were killed, Captain Willis, Captain Llewellyn and 2nd Lieutenants Hone and Sweeting being wounded at the same time. The ground gained was, however, successfully held for the time being. The effect of this advance was to give a slightly concave formation to the eastern face of the Ypres salient, the two extremities now projecting beyond the centre trenches in the Polygon wood. This curious formation, however, was very temporary, both of the horns so formed having shortly to withdraw. The withdrawal of the southern horn was begun on the night of the 26th, during the events already narrated. We may now consider the subsequent events which led to its complete disappearance.

In the very small hours of the same morning on which the 6th Brigade advanced—before daylight, in fact—the 1st Scots Guards marched down the Menin road to resume its place in the 1st Brigade. At Gheluvelt the battalion deployed to the north of the road, and at once came under the blind shell-fire which ceased not night or day in this particular area. Captain Hamilton and Captain Balfour were killed, and Lieutenants Wickham and Roberts wounded. The battalion, however, worked its way up to its position on the left of the 1st Coldstream, and there awaited events. How dramatic those events were destined to prove was little suspected at the time.

A few hours later the 20th Brigade, returning from its one night's rest in the outskirts of Ypres, followed them down the same road, and filed into the shelter-trenches south of the road. Here they stayed till 5 p.m. on the 28th, when they continued their march down the high road through Gheluvelt, and took over the trenches just west and south of the Kruiseik cross-roads.

Here for the moment we may leave them in order to take a glance at the general situation.

The day which followed, that is to say October 29th, was the first of the five days during which the Kaiser was present in person with his troops opposite Ypres. He had arrived with the avowed intention of stimulating the army to one supreme, irresistible effort which would carry all before it, and open the coveted road to Calais to the mass of troops now concentrated at Roulers and Menin.

The occasion was signalized on the morning of the 29th by a grand assault along and on each side of the Menin road. This broad highroad was the most direct and obvious route to Ypres, and the Germans—as their way is—went straight for the shortest cut. There was no secret about the enterprise; it was, in fact, known among all ranks of the British army, and even published in some of the general orders of the evening before, that the XXVII. German Reserve Corps would attack Kruiseik and Zandvoorde at 5.30 a.m. on the 29th.

In the light of this general knowledge, subsequent events are not wholly easy to understand. The attack came at the very hour which had been announced, and—as far as Kruiseik was concerned—at the very spot. Zandvoorde, as a matter of fact, was not implicated, and so can be left out of the discussion.

At Kruiseik our line of defence was just in rear of the cross-roads, about a quarter of a mile nearer Ypres than it had been on the 26th. The six regiments in the front line which came in the path of the attack were the 1st Grenadiers, 2nd Gordons and 2nd

Scots Fusiliers south of the road, and the Black Watch, 1st Coldstream and 1st Scots Guards to the north of it. In reserve were the 2nd Scots Guards and the Border Regiment, the latter being in Gheluvelt, the former to the south of it.

At 5.30 then, with true military punctuality, the Germans made their advance under cover of a thick fog, and, as subsequent events proved, succeeded in getting past and behind our first line without opposition. It is said that they marched in column of fours straight down the main Menin road, which, for some reason only known to staff officers, does not appear to have been in the charge of any of the first line troops.

However that may be, the fact remains that the Germans did get past, without a shot being fired from either side, and established their machine-guns in the houses along the roadside in rear; with the result that the regiments next the road suddenly found themselves, without any warning, assailed by a murderous machine-gun fire from both rear and flank. To add to the unpleasantness of the situation, they were at the same time vigorously shelled by our own artillery. Under this combined attack the 1st Grenadiers next the road on the south side suffered very severely. Colonel Earle was wounded almost at the first discharge, and Major Stucley, who then took over command, was killed within a short interval. Owing to the thickness of the fog it was a matter of great difficulty to locate the enemy with any degree of accuracy, or to return a fire which appeared to come from the direction of our own reserves. Captain Rasch, who was now in command, accordingly decided to withdraw the battalion into the woods to the south, leaving the enemy to continue their fusillade at the empty trenches. With them went the left flank company of the Gordons, under Captain Burnett. "C" Company of the Gordons, which was on the right of Captain Burnett's company, was comparatively clear of the fire from the rear, and did not withdraw with the others. The subsequent exploits of this company were most remarkable, and will be described later on.

The fog now suddenly lifted, the sun came through, and the situation became comparatively clear to both sides. The Germans ceased their fusillade from behind at the empty trenches, and began to press southwards from the road, and westward from the direction of Menin, in great numbers. To meet this new movement, the 1st Grenadiers and Captain Burnett's company of the Gordons formed up and charged, driving the enemy back to the road in considerable disorder. In the moment of victory, however, they were heavily enfiladed from the trenches recently occupied by Captain Burnett's company, and numbers fell. They were again forced to withdraw to the south, the enemy following close on their heels. Once more the Grenadiers and Gordons reformed, and once more they drove the enemy back to the road, only to be themselves again driven back by weight of numbers. It was at this moment that Lieutenant Brooke, of the Gordon Highlanders, who had been sent from the right flank with a message, arrived on the scene and—seeing the overwhelming superiority in numbers of the enemy—hurriedly collected a handful of men from the rear (servants, cooks, orderlies, etc.), and led them forward in a gallant attempt to do something towards equalizing numbers. He and nearly all his men were killed, but he was subsequently awarded the Victoria Cross for his action.

In the meanwhile the Grenadiers were fighting to a finish. Refusing to be beaten or to give way, they fought up to the moment when the order arrived for them to retire to Gheluvelt. This was about 10 a.m. By that time 500 out of the 650 men who had gone into action had fallen, and out of the sixteen officers only four were left. No. 4 Company—the heroes of the successful charge on the 24th—alone lost 200 men, or, in other words, were wiped out.

Of the officers, Major Stucley, Captain Rennie, Lord R. Wellesley, the Hon. W. Forester and the Hon. A. Douglas-Pennant were killed, in addition to which Colonel Earle, the Hon. C. Ponsonby, Lieutenants Lambert, Kenyon-Slaney and Powell were wounded. Lieutenant Butt, the medical officer attached, was killed while dressing Colonel Earle's wounds. The casualties of the Gordons were between two and three hundred.

While this had been going on south of the road, an almost identical state of things prevailed on the north side where were stationed the Black Watch and 1st Coldstream. These two battalions similarly found themselves, without any warning, mowed down in the fog by machine-gun fire from their rear and right flank. Gradually they too were forced back, fighting every yard of the way, but powerless to stem the masses of the enemy opposed to them. Both these battalions were practically annihilated. The 1st Coldstream battalion, in fact, may be said to have ceased to exist, for the time being, after this day. The remnant was shortly afterwards absorbed into the 2nd and 3rd Battalions. That remnant consisted of 180 rank and file; *no officers* and no senior N.C.O.

The right flank company of the 1st Scots Guards shared the fate of the two battalions on its right. It became isolated, was surrounded by masses of the enemy, and ceased to exist.

At 11 a.m. the 2nd Scots Fusiliers, who had been on the right of the Gordons, and just outside of the pressure of the first attack, had in their turn to fall back, Colonel Uniacke with two companies of the Gordons going forward again to aid them in their retirement.

About noon things were looking pretty serious; the Germans were pressing on towards Gheluvelt in great numbers, both on the main road itself and to the north and south of it, and it seemed doubtful whether their impetus could be checked.

At this critical moment, a succession of incidents, small in themselves, but powerful as a combination, brought about a marked change in the fortunes of the day. It has already been mentioned that "C" Company of the Gordons, under Captain R. S. Gordon, had remained throughout the morning in its original trenches, the order to retire not having reached it. Curiously enough, another small detachment to its right was in a very similar position. This detachment consisted of a platoon of the 2nd Queen's, and about a hundred men of other units, under the command of Major Bottomley of the Queen's. The party had been sent forward to reinforce the 20th Brigade, and, at the time of the retirement, was in some dug-outs in a very advanced position on the high ground near Kruiseik. As in the case of "C" Company of the Gordons, the order to retire did not reach them, and they were left. Here then were two distinct and quite independent detachments, completely isolated, and cut off by a good half mile from the rest of the brigade. It seemed as though their destruction was a foregone conclusion. In the event, however, not only were they not destroyed, but they were able, from their unsuspected positions, to work very considerable havoc in the ranks of the enemy. It so happened that Major Bottomley's party contained an unusual number of marksmen, including Lieutenant Wilson of the 2nd Queen's. These—

quite regardless of their own perilous position, or of the fire which they were sure to draw upon themselves by their action—now laid themselves out to take advantage of their advanced position to pick off the Germans to right and left. The very audacity of the proceeding proved their saving, the enemy finding it very hard to properly locate a fire which seemed to come from their very midst. There was, however, some retaliation, and Lieutenant Wilson was eventually shot through the head and killed.

It cannot well be claimed that sniping such as this—however effective—had any appreciable influence on the tide of battle, but this claim can be justly made in the case of "C" Company of the 2nd Gordons. This company's presence was equally unsuspected by the enemy, and, soon after midday, a German battalion proceeded to mass in close column within 300 yards of its position. Such a target was of course unmissable, and within five minutes the German battalion was annihilated, 850 dead and wounded being afterwards found on the spot where it had concentrated.

It is satisfactory to be able to record that both these gallant detachments successfully withdrew. Captain Gordon remained in his position till dusk, when, by exercising great care, he succeeded in rejoining his battalion. Major Bottomley actually remained in his position till the night of the following day, *i.e.*, the 30th, when he succeeded in safely extricating his party from their perilous position—a truly astonishing performance in view of the fact that the Germans were not only round him, but were in actual occupation of the trenches to right and left.

While this was taking place south of the road, the 1st Scots Guards, north of the road, were gradually bringing about a change in the aspect of the fight. It will be remembered that the two battalions between them and the road, *viz.*, the Black Watch and 1st Coldstream, had been engulfed and overwhelmed in the German advance, a fate which had also overtaken Captain de la Pasture's company of the 1st Scots Guards, which was on the right of that battalion. In this crisis—for it was undoubtedly an extremely critical moment—Captain Stephen, with a quick grasp of the situation, brought up the reserve company of the Scots Guards, together with some stragglers from the 1st Coldstream who had escaped the carnage on the right. Facing his command half right, he proceeded to pour volley after volley into the flank of the Germans pressing forward between him and the road. Some of the Germans turned to face this new attack, but the Guardsmen, fighting with superb courage, held them off throughout the afternoon. During this memorable performance on the part of Captain Stephen's company, the company commander himself and Sir G. Ogilvy were killed, and the Hon. G. Macdonald and Sir V. Mackenzie wounded. The 1st Scots Guards had now lost 10 officers and 370 men since they had marched down the Menin road two days before.[1] The battalion received great praise in high quarters for the part it had played at this critical moment in the fortunes of the day, and there can be little doubt that the tremendous losses they had inflicted on the enemy had appreciably checked the German advance.

Captain Gordon's attack had taken the enemy on the left flank, and Captain Stephen's on the right flank. They were yet to meet a still more severe check from in front. In partial reserve on the hill on which Gheluvelt stands, were detachments of the 2nd Gordon Highlanders, 2nd Scots Guards, 2nd Queen's, S. Wales Borderers and the Border Regiment. It was about midday when the Germans, having forced their way as described through the regiments next the Menin road, began pushing forward towards Gheluvelt, the main body marching in column of fours along the road from Gheluvelt itself, where the main road passes through the village, the head of the advancing column was out of sight, owing to a bend in the road at the foot of the hill. Captain Watson, however, who was in charge of the machine-gun section of the Border Regiment, managed to get a couple of maxims through a ploughed field into some turnips on the north slope of the hill. From here there was a clear view of the road stretching away to Kruiseik, with the head of the German column about 1,200 yards distant. On to this column both machine-guns were now trained. The position was ideal for working execution on the enemy, but it was in no way entrenched, and fully exposed to the enemy's fire. The head of the enemy's column was soon knocked to pieces, and, on the other hand, one of the Border Regiment machine-guns was knocked out, but the other kept going till all the ammunition was expended. In the meanwhile

---

1. Up to the end of January, 1915, the total casualties in the two battalions Scots Guards amounted to 2,888 of all ranks.

the German infantry advancing south of the road had become visible to the several detachments afore-mentioned, of whom Major Craufurd of the Gordons had assumed temporary command, and these now opened a galling fire on the advancing ranks, which they succeeded in throwing into considerable confusion.

This moment proved the turning-point in the day's battle. The frontal fire from the Border Regiment's machine-guns and the above-named detachments, coupled with the enfilading fire from the 1st Scots Guards to the north of the road, brought the advancing force to a standstill, which—when the reserves from Gheluvelt were advanced—quickly developed into a retreat. The Germans fell back to Kruiseik, which they occupied, and which from this date on remained in their hands. The 3rd Brigade was brought forward to occupy the place of the Black Watch and 1st Coldstream north of the road, the 1st Scots Guards and the Camerons retaining their original morning position.

This battle of the Kruiseik cross-roads had cost us very dear, some of the finest battalions in the British army being practically annihilated, but there can be no question but that the losses of the attacking forces were incomparably greater. It must be borne in mind that the British forces which actually took part in this fight numbered at the outside 5,000, while the attacking force consisted of an entire army corps, that is to say, approximately, 24,000 infantry.

It may be interesting at this point, at the risk of forestalling matters a little, to explain the gradual process of retirement by which our line was straightened, and the bulge eliminated from our defensive position. It is less easy to explain why the process was so gradual. We may take our furthest advance east to have been on the 19th. On that date the 22nd Brigade pushed forward as far as the Roulers-Menin railway. There, however, they encountered very strong opposition, and withdrew to Zonnebeke—a distance of six miles—on the same day. The 20th Brigade, however, did not take part in this retirement, and entrenched themselves at the point to which they had advanced, east of Kruiseik.

On the 24th the 6th Brigade made a second advance south of the Zonnebeke road; and on the following day the Guards' Brigade fought its way up into line on the right of the 6th Brigade, while the 5th and 1st Brigades filled the gap between the Guards' Brigade and the 20th Brigade at Kruiseik. These several advances resulted in a line of defence which jutted out from Zonnebeke to Reutel, and then—after passing east of Kruiseik and Zandvoorde—fell back quite suddenly, and in an all but straight line, to Klein Zillebeke. Klein Zillebeke, and Zonnebeke, then, were the starting-points to north and south of the bulge, and it is significant that these two points have never been lost; nor has our ultimate middle-of-November line, which ran along the high ridge connecting these two places, ever been forced. But till this obvious line of defence was reached, we lost ground on each occasion that the enemy attacked in force.

On the 26th we were driven back from east of Kruiseik to a position west of Kruiseik; on the 29th we lost Kruiseik and were driven back to Gheluvelt; on the 30th we lost Zandvoorde; and on the 31st we lost Gheluvelt, and were driven back to a new position nearer Veldhoek. On November 2nd we were driven from this position, and our line was retired another 300 yards towards Hooge. Here it remained till November 11th, when the Prussian Guard captured this position, but was unable to drive us from the Veldhoek ridge. This ridge has, from that date to the present moment, proved the *ne plus ultra* of German advance, and it is fairly safe to predict that it will so remain to the end, unless voluntarily relinquished for sanitary or strategic reasons. This in itself is a cause for congratulation and even triumph, but not so is the thought of the many good men who laid down their lives between Kruiseik and Veldhoek in the defence of the indefensible.

In reckoning up these successive retirements from the point of view of military failure or success, or from the, perhaps, more interesting point of view of the relative fighting merits of those who retired and those who advanced, it is well to realize, from the start, the tremendous disparity in numbers and freshness of the opposing forces. The British commanders had, throughout this defence of Ypres, to ring the changes, as between reserve and firing line, with battalions, and sometimes even with companies. The German commanders could afford to do it with army corps.

Day after day, the same British battalions, jaded, depleted of officers, and gradually dwindling into mere skeletons, were called upon to withstand the attacks of fresh and fresh troops. It was not merely that the Germans had the superiority in numbers on each occasion when they attacked. This, of course, must always be the privilege of the attacking side; but they had also the unspeakable advantage of being able at any time to direct a stream of fresh troops against any given part of our thin, weary, battered line. Thus on October 29th the XXVII. Reserve Corps attacked Kruiseik; on the 30th the XV. Army Corps attacked Zandvoorde; on October 31st and November 1st we had the XIII., XXIV., and II. Bavarian Corps attacking the line from the Menin road to Messines, to which on November 2nd must be added the XXVI. Army Corps. By this time, however, the 16th French Army had come up, and did something towards equalizing matters.

But again on November 11th, fifteen fresh battalions of the Prussian Guard were brought up, and all that Sir Douglas Haig had to put in their path were the remnants of the same unconquerable battalions that had now been fighting, without intermission, for close on three months.

CHAPTER 26

Zandvoorde

Following the loss of Kruiseik on the 29th came the loss of Zandvoorde on the 30th. The particular section in the line of defence known as the Zandvoorde trenches had from first to last been a death-trap, and had proved particularly expensive to the 3rd Cavalry Division, whose special privilege it had been to defend them. They curved round the south-east side of the village, following the contours of the ridge, and, being the most prominent feature in the entire Ypres salient, were particularly susceptible to shell-fire from all quarters, except the north. Their chief attraction, from the purely military point of view, lay in the fact that they were on the crest of a ridge some 120 feet high, which here juts out into the plain, and which faces the ridge of about the same height a mile and a quarter away, on which Kruiseik stands. Their weakness lay in the fact that they were practically surrounded by the enemy, and were even open to attack from the direction of Hollebeke, which lay due west of their southern extension. In these circumstances their loss on the 30th was not wholly a matter for regret.

At the moment of the final attack, the 7th C.B. (Household Cavalry) had already been in these trenches for three days and nights, under a ceaseless shell-fire from south and east, and occasionally even from west. In the case of the machine-gun section of the Blues, under Lord Worsley, that period was doubled, the detachment having been in the advance trenches for six days and nights unrelieved.

There is reason to believe that the supreme attack on Zandvoorde had originally been planned for the 29th, so as to take place simultaneously with that on Kruiseik, but a delay in the arrival of the XV. German Army Corps resulted in its postponement till the following day. The expected reinforcements arrived during the night of the 29th and—all being now according to arrangement—the attack took place at daybreak on the following morning.

The attack took the form of a storm of shrapnel and high-explosives of so terrific a nature that by nine o'clock the Household Cavalry trenches had been literally blown to pieces, and the brigade was forced to retire slowly down the hill, keeping up a covering fire as it went. The retirement was effected in good order, but Lord Hugh Grosvenor's squadron of the 1st Life Guards, "C" Squadron of the 2nd Life Guards, and Lord Worsley's machine-gun section of the Blues did not succeed in withdrawing with the rest of the brigade, and their fate is still a matter of uncertainty. It is probable, however, that, in the pandemonium which was reigning, the order to retire did not reach them, and that those who survived the bombardment awaited the infantry attack which followed, and fought it out to an absolute finish. An officer in the R. Welsh Fusiliers' trenches, on the left of the Zandvoorde trenches, subsequently described the defence put up that day by the Household Cavalry as one of the finest feats of the war. It may well be that untold deeds of heroism remain yet to be recorded in connection with that morning's work.[1]

The R. Welsh Fusiliers were on the right of the 22nd Brigade and on the left of the Household Cavalry, in trenches which curved back from the Zandvoorde trenches and faced in the main northwest, whereas the Zandvoorde trenches faced south-east. These trenches were at the best ill-constructed affairs, and were weakened in the middle by a big gap where the road from Zandvoorde to Becelaere passed through them.

The Zandvoorde trenches passed into the hands of the enemy soon after nine, and the Germans at once swarmed into them and began making their way along towards the north, till they reached a position from which they could get the Welsh Fusiliers in flank. Then began the annihilation of this very gallant regiment. From

---

1. Among those missing on that morning was the Hon. Francis Lambton. He was subsequently reported to have been killed.

the moment that the Zandvoorde trenches went, its position was hopeless, its right flank being completely unprotected, and its own trenches disconnected and ill-adapted for mutual protection. The regiment, however, fought as it had fought on the 19th and again on the 20th and 21st. It fought, in the words of the C. in C., "till every officer had been killed or wounded; only ninety men rejoined the brigade." As a matter of fact, the exact number of survivors out of a battalion which a fortnight earlier had numbered 1,100 was 86, and these were shortly afterwards absorbed into the 2nd Queen's, their only remaining officer being the quartermaster.

Among those that fell on that day were Captain Barker, Colonel Cadogan and his Adjutant, Lieutenant Dooner. The latter was killed in a very gallant attempt to cross the interval which divided the trenches, and investigate the state of affairs on the right; and the colonel fell in an equally gallant attempt to rescue his subordinate after he had fallen.

The position was now—as may be supposed—extremely serious, the enemy being in complete possession of the Zandvoorde ridge. The 7th C.B. (Household Cavalry), when it had fallen back in the morning, had retired through the 6th C.B. and formed up in rear.

Its retreat had been greatly assisted by the magnificent work of the two Horse Artillery Batteries attached, *viz.*, "C" Battery, under Major White, and "K" Battery, under Major Lamont. Both displayed the greatest daring and activity, and the latter succeeded in completely knocking out a German battery which was just coming into action on the Zandvoorde ridge.

In the meanwhile, the only force which stood in the way of the enemy was the 6th C.B., that is to say, three cavalry regiments, all considerably weakened by fighting. The gravity of the situation lay in the fact that if the Klein Zillebeke position went, there was nothing further to prevent the enemy marching straight into Ypres, only three miles distant, in which case the 1st A.C. and 7th Division would have been irretrievably cut off from their base and supplies, and the capture or annihilation of these three divisions would have inevitably followed.

Accordingly Sir Douglas Haig, quick to realize that the events of the next few hours would decide the making or marring of the campaign, sent out an ultimatum to the effect that the line to which we had now been driven, *i.e.*, from Gheluvelt to the corner of the canal north of Hollebeke, was to be held at all costs. Concurrently an urgent appeal was sent to General Allenby to send up with all possible speed any and all regiments available. Allenby sent the Scots Greys and the 3rd and 4th Hussars—all from different brigades. The Greys and the 3rd Hussars arrived first on the scene, and passed across to the left flank of the 6th C.B., filling up, in fact, the gap between that brigade and General Bulfin's (2nd) Brigade on its left. The 4th Hussars, who had further to come, arrived in time to take up a position on the right of the Royals (who were the right-hand regiment of the 6th C.B.), and carry on the line of defence beyond the railway. The position then was that the line of the three regiments of the 6th C.B. was extended by the 3rd Hussars and Greys on the left, and by the 4th Hussars on the right.

The 7th C.B., who had concentrated at the little village of Zwartelen in rear of the 6th C.B., now sent off two squadrons of the Blues to support the Royals, who were holding the *château* at Hollebeke. This château lies on the low ground to the east of the canal, whereas Hollebeke itself is on the west side. The *château* was considerably in advance of the line which was ordered to be held, and with Zandvoorde gone was of no strategic importance. This combined force held off the enemy for some hours, during which time Sergeant McLellan, of the Royals, especially distinguished himself by several acts of great gallantry, but by midday the *château* had to be abandoned and was occupied by German infantry. Except for this loss, the cavalry line held its ground throughout the day. There was no further infantry attack, but it had to stand a severe shelling all through the afternoon, and its casualties were numerous, among those of the 10th Hussars being Captain Kinkead, Captain Fielden, Captain Stewart and the Hon. H. Baring.

The R. Sussex, too, in General Bulfin's 2nd Brigade, on the left of the cavalry, came in for their full share of the bombardment and suffered very severely, Colonel Crispin and Lieutenants Croft, Marillier and Lousada being killed.

At five o'clock in the afternoon the five cavalry regiments

were relieved by Lord Cavan's Brigade, the 2nd Grenadier Guards under Major Lord Bernard Lennox[2] taking over the position on the canal—later on to become famous under the name of Hill 60, while the Irish Guards continued the line on their left. The line was still further strengthened on the following morning by the addition of the Oxfordshire Light Infantry from the 5th Brigade, and the 2nd Gordon Highlanders from the 20th Brigade, these two battalions being added to General Bulfin's command, which was on the left of Lord Cavan's.

2. Killed November, 1914.

CHAPTER 27

Gheluvelt

October 31st may be said to have witnessed the supreme effort of the enemy to break through to Ypres. The attack on this day was pressed simultaneously along the whole of our front from Messines to the Menin road, and lasted not only throughout the day but during the greater part of the night. This tremendous battle, covering as it did a frontage of twelve miles, can only be adequately described by cutting it up into three sections, the first of which deals with the fight along the Menin road, the second with the struggle at Klein Zillebeke, and the third with the attack on the cavalry corps at Wytschate and Messines.

We will deal first with the fight on the Menin road. Here, it will be remembered, our troops had been forced back on the 29th from a line just west of Kruiseik cross-roads to the Gheluvelt trenches, three-quarters of a mile further back, and on the higher ridge on which that village stands.

On the morning of the 31st the new position was in its turn attacked, and under conditions which in many ways recalled the fight of two days before. There was, however, this difference, that, while the attack of the 29th had been in the nature of a surprise in the fog, and had been unheralded by any previous cannonade, that of the 31st was preceded by a bombardment which, in point of violence, threw into the shade everything which the campaign had yet witnessed. The expenditure of ammunition must have been colossal. This terrific discharge of missiles commenced at daybreak, and gradually increased in volume up to eleven o'clock, when it ceased and the infantry attack commenced.

The shell-fire had been mainly focussed on the 3rd and 22nd Brigades in the neighbourhood of Gheluvelt. By the association of these two brigades, the 1st and 2nd battalions of the Queen's (R. West Surrey Regiment) for the first time in history found themselves fighting side by side. The occasion was an historic one, but not without a strong note of tragedy, both battalions being in the direct track of the bombardment, and suffering very severely. Each battalion, too, lost its C.O. during the morning, Colonel Pell of the 1st Battalion being killed and Colonel Coles of the 2nd Battalion wounded.

The tactics of the enemy in these Menin road attacks almost always took the same form. All the batteries within the area would concentrate on the road and on the trenches immediately to right and left of the road, making these positions absolutely untenable. Then, when the troops in the track of the shell-fire had fallen back dazed into semi-unconsciousness by the inferno, they would drive a dense mass of infantry into the gap, and so enfilade—and very often surround—the trenches which were still occupied to right and left of the gap. By this method, companies, and some-times whole battalions, which had stuck out the shell-fire, were overwhelmed and annihilated.

Such a fate on this occasion overtook the right flank company of the South Wales Borderers just north of Gheluvelt. This com-pany formed the northern boundary of the gap caused by the bombardment, and the German wedge, spreading out towards the right, bore down on it from three sides. Major Lawrence, in command of the company, faced half the men about and kept up the fight to the bitter end, but it was merely a question of selling their lives as dearly as possible. The tide swept over them and they ceased to exist.

The remaining companies of the South Wales Borderers man-aged to maintain their ground till the line north of the road was re-established in the following way.

At 1.30 the 2nd Worcestershire Regiment, who were in re-serve at the six cross-roads at the corner of the Polygon wood, a mile to the rear, were ordered to retake the lost position. This they did in the following very gallant manner, led by Major Hankey. They deployed in the woods just to the rear of Gheluvelt, and, advancing in a series of short rushes, charged right up to the line of the lost trenches. The last rush had to be made across 200 yards of open ground in the face of a terrific shrapnel fire. Over 100 of the Worcesters fell in this last rush, but the remainder charged home and drove out the Germans with heavy loss. The old trenches were found to have been filled in, but a sunken road just in rear provided fair cover, and this the Worcesters now lined, joining up their left with the right of the South Wales Borderers. The Germans, however, were still in the village itself and the position was at best a precarious one. They managed, however, to hold on till dark.

The Worcesters lost 187 men in this short, brilliant charge. The achievement was alluded to by the C. in C. as one of the finest in the whole campaign, and one which saved the army from a very awkward predicament.

The 1st Scots Guards, on the left of the South Wales Borderers again, as on the 29th, stood firm throughout the day, and contributed in no small measure to the ultimate repulse of the enemy. In the afternoon one company of this battalion was detached to co-operate in the counter-attack made by the Worcesters, and generally to re-establish the broken line north of Gheluvelt. This they succeeded in doing, with very able support from the 42nd Battery R.F.A., but in the doing of it lost Captain Wickham and Major Vandeweyer, the former of whom was killed.

Meanwhile another historic resistance was being put up south of the road by the 2nd R. Scots Fusiliers. This battalion formed the southern boundary of the gap, just as the South Wales Borderers formed the northern boundary; and when the German infantry wedge was forced in, it found its trenches very badly raked from the gardens of the château, where the enemy had installed some machine-guns. General Watt, the brigadier, recognizing that the position of this regiment had now become untenable, telephoned through to them to retire. The wire, however, had been cut by shrapnel and the message did not arrive. Two orderlies were thereupon successively dispatched to order their retirement. Both were knocked over and again the order did not reach. In the meanwhile, Colonel Baird Smith, having received no order to retire, continued to hold his ground with ever dwindling numbers, till in the end the German masses swept over them, and another gallant British battalion ceased to exist. Only seventy men, commanded by a junior officer, escaped the carnage of that day.

Five months later, General Watt, addressing the officers and men at Sailly, after another great performance by the same battalion, said with reference to this occasion: "Colonel Baird Smith, gallant soldier that he was, decided and rightly to hold his ground, and the R. Scots Fusiliers fought and fought till the Germans absolutely surrounded them and swarmed into the trenches. I think it was perfectly splendid. Mind you, it was no case of 'hands up' or any nonsense of that sort; it was a fight to a finish. You may well be proud to belong to such a regiment and I am proud to have you in my brigade."

To the south of the R. Scots Fusiliers, and in the same brigade, were the 2nd Bedfords. This regiment, too, had suffered very severely during the day, both its senior officers, Major Traill and Major Stares, being killed, but the brigade order to retire had not failed to reach it, as in the case of the Scotchmen, and it had been able to effect its withdrawal in good order.

The Germans did not carry their advance beyond Gheluvelt. The ground they had gained had only been won by a prodigious expenditure of ammunition, followed by a reckless sacrifice of men, and their losses had been enormous. Their further progress, too, was barred by the troops which had been shelled out of the village in the morning. These were now formed up half facing the road between Gheluvelt and Veldhoek, and offered a successful bar to any further advance on the part of the enemy. The Germans, however, did not relinquish their attempts to push on to Veldhoek without further serious fighting, in the course of which the 2nd Queen's sustained still further losses, their three senior officers, Colonel Coles, Major Croft and Major Bottomley falling wounded, as well as Captain Weeding and Lieutenant Philpot. Night fell without any further advance on the part of the enemy. Gheluvelt itself, however, in spite of the gallant counter-attack north of the road, during the afternoon, may be considered as having been lost from this day on.

CHAPTER 28

Messines and Wytschate

In order to avoid the confusion inseparable from a constant change of scene, it will be best to deal briefly now with the doings at Messines and Wytschate, after which the Klein Zillebeke section can monopolize our attention up to the close of this little chronicle. In order to pick up the thread where it was dropped, it will be necessary to go back to the 30th. On that day General Allenby wired to headquarters that his numbers were too weak to hold his position from the canal at Hollebeke to the La Doune stream, south of Messines, for long unaided, and the C. in C. at once responded by sending up four battalions from the 2nd A.C. under General Shaw to his assistance. These, as will presently be seen, arrived in the very nick of time to save the situation. Pending their arrival, the cavalry had a truly colossal task before them. They were absurdly outnumbered; they had opposed to them, in the XXIV. and II. Bavarian Corps, some of the finest fighters in the German Army, stimulated by the presence of the Kaiser himself, and they were engaged in a form of warfare to which they had never been trained. French reinforcements were being hurried up, it is true, but it was reckoned that, at the earliest, they could not arrive in less than forty-eight hours. During these forty-eight hours, could the cavalry, with the assistance which had been sent up from the 2nd A.C., successfully oppose the pressure of two army corps? This was the problem of the moment. We know now that it did succeed in doing so, but even with this fact behind us as a matter of history, we may still—in view of the extraordinary disparity in numbers— wonder as to how it was done.

First let us deal with Messines, which was almost on the southern boundary of the Cavalry Corps position. Here we find posted the 1st and 2nd C.B., or, to be more exact, these two brigades were in the trenches to the east of that town, the Bays being on the north side, then the 9th Lancers and 4th Dragoon Guards, with the 5th Dragoon Guards to the south. In reserve, in the second line, were the 18th and 11th Hussars. The latter regiment had suffered severely from the bombardment on the previous day, their trenches being completely blown in and many men buried and killed. Amongst the officers, Lieutenants Chaytor and Lawson-Smith had been killed, and Lieutenant-Colonel Pitman, Major Anderson and the Hon. C. Mulholland wounded. Again, on the following day, the regiment lost a very fine athlete, and a champion boxer, in Captain Halliday, who was killed by a shell near the convent.

In spite of an appalling bombardment, the regiments in the front line held on all through the night of the 30th, and up to midday on the 31st. Then they began to be gradually driven back, and by 2 p.m. they were all in the town. The retirement was effected in perfect order. Corporal Seaton, 9th Lancers, behaved with extraordinary courage during this movement and was recommended for the Victoria Cross. With the idea of helping the withdrawal of his regiment, he remained absolutely alone in his trench working his machine-gun till the enemy were within twenty yards. Incredible as it may appear, he then managed, thanks to great coolness and presence of mind, to rejoin his regiment unwounded.

Once in the town, the cavalry lined the houses of the main street from end to end, and there awaited developments. These took the form of a cessation of the shelling and a very determined attempt on the part of the Bavarians to take the town. They failed, however, to get across the square, being shot down in numbers from the windows of the houses opposite. A second and more carefully thought-out attack followed later, and it is doubtful how this might have ended but for the opportune arrival of the K.O.S.B. and the K.O.Y.L.I., one at each end of the town. This reinforcement once more turned the scale against the Bavarians, and for the second time they were driven back. Both the infantry battalions engaged, in the words of General Allenby to Sir Horace, "fought magnificently," but the K.O.Y.L.I. lost its

CO., Colonel King, who was killed while leading that regiment to the attack. The respite of the cavalry was short. The enemy was in over-powering force and they were not to be denied. They now proceeded for five solid hours to shell the place with every conceivable species of projectile known to warfare. At 2 a.m. on the 31st the infantry attacked for the third time.

In the meanwhile the only available reserve was being hurried up from Neuve Eglise, as fast as motor-buses could bring it. This was the London Scottish, which had arrived at the front the day previous, after having been employed for some weeks at the base. They reached Messines during the preliminary bombardment on the night of the 30th, and, before going into action, were split up, half of the battalion joining up with the K.O.S.B. at one end of the town, and the rest with the K.O.Y.L.I. at the other. There was a full moon and a clear sky, and it was as light as day, and it has been said that for picturesque effect no incident in the war has equalled that night attack on Messines. An additional interest was lent to the scene by the fact that the London Scottish were the first Territorial battalion to be in action, and there was some speculation as to how their conduct would compare with that of the Regulars. It is now a matter of history that they acquitted themselves as well as the most tried troops, and that under exceptionally trying circumstances. If it be true that casualties in killed and wounded are the barometer of a regiment's intrepidity, then they indeed register high in the scale, for they lost 9 officers and 400 men in that first night's fighting. In any event they rendered very valuable service in an acute emergency, and it is on record that in a hand to hand bayonet encounter with the Bavarians, they actually drove those noted warriors back. The odds, however, were altogether too great against the little British force, and on the morning of November 1st Messines passed into the hands of the enemy.

A feat so remarkable as to rival the deeds of Shaw, the Lifeguardsman, was performed by Sergeant-Major Wright, of the Carabineers, during this defence of Messines. This N.C.O., while carrying a message to headquarters, found his path blocked by a part of the enemy. Without a moment's hesitation he charged them and cut his way through, killing five. Another Carabineer who behaved with repeated gallantry during these operations was Private Meston, and both he and Sergeant-Major Wright were given the D.C.M.

On the same night, *i.e.*, the night of October 31st, Wytschate shared the fate of Messines.

The 4th C.B. had succeeded in holding this place throughout the day, but during the course of the night they found themselves very hard pressed, and were gradually forced back. In this emergency the Northumberland Fusiliers and Lincolns were ordered up to the support of the cavalry.

These two 9th Brigade battalions had arrived at Kemmel during the afternoon, having marched that day from Estaires, a distance of some twelve miles. They were in billets, resting after their hard day's work, when the message arrived, about one o'clock in the morning, to the effect that they were required. Within an hour from the receipt of the message both battalions were on the road, the Lincolns being the first to arrive on the scene of action. The country was totally unknown to the newcomers, but a cavalry sergeant was met who volunteered to lead them to the position occupied by the enemy. Under his guidance they entered the cutting through which the light railway, which runs along the edge of the road from Kemmel to Wytschate, passes just before it reaches the town. Here they became aware of a number of men moving in their direction, who called out in excellent English and Hindustani that they were British cavalry and Indians. Before the actual identity of these men could, in the gloom of the night, be ascertained for certain, the newcomers opened fire, both from the end of the cutting and from the sides; and the Lincolns, who were closely packed in the narrow defile, fell in numbers before they could be extricated. After getting clear, they met the Northumberland Fusiliers advancing from the direction of Kemmel, and together the two battalions formed up, and with great gallantry once more attacked the entrance to the town. The inequality in numbers, however, was too great. The Germans were literally swarming in the town, and it was clear that General Shaw's two battalions had been set to an impossible task. They retired to the outskirts of the town, where they held on till daylight, lying in the open fields. When dawn broke the London Scottish could be seen on their right, but no troops on their left.

The unpleasantness of the situation was not in any way relieved by a heavy fire which our own artillery now opened upon the two battalions, under the mistaken impression that they were Germans. Many men were killed and wounded by this fire. In conformity with the general plan of retiring to the Wulverghem road, the Lincolns and Northumberland Fusiliers were now withdrawn, and Wytschate went the way of Messines. The Lincolns lost 400 men and all but 4 officers during this short night attack. Colonel W. E. Smith was specially commended for the great personal courage which he showed during the attack, and for the skill with which he ultimately withdrew his regiment. Lieutenant Blackwood was awarded the D.S.O. for very gallantly continuing to lead the attack after every officer senior to himself had fallen. The losses of the Northumberland Fusiliers were not quite so heavy, but were still very severe, especially in officers.

The dismounted cavalry line now retired to the Wulverghem to Kemmel road, where they entrenched themselves, but their numbers were quite inadequate for the frontage to be held. Pending the arrival of the French, Sir Horace was ordered by the C. in C. to send up to their assistance every available man from the 2nd A.C., which was recouping at Pradelles. The Dorsets and Worcesters were accordingly sent to Neuve Eglise, and the remaining seven and a half battalions—all skeletons—were sent up to east of Bailleul under General Morland. Such was the position on November 1st.

On this day the anxiously awaited 16th French Army began to arrive, the troops being railed up at the rate of eighty train loads a day, and at 11 a.m. on the 2nd, both Messines and Wytschate were retaken by the French with some assistance from our cavalry. Some of the 12th Lancers, led by 2nd Lieutenant Williams, of the Scots Greys, made a very brilliant bayonet charge during the recapture of the latter town. The above-mentioned officer was officially reported to have himself killed eleven Germans on this occasion, and was awarded the D.S.O.

The French now officially took over from us the line from Messines on the south to the canal on the north. It is interesting to note that, between October 27th and November 11th, some 200,000 French infantry, twenty regiments of cavalry and sixty pieces of heavy artillery reached Ypres, Poperinghe, and Bailleul. It is difficult to conceive of any more eloquent tribute to the astonishing performance of the thin little khaki ribbon, which had for a fortnight wound round Ypres, than the fact that this great force was found none too strong to hold one fourth of the front over which our handful of men had so far successfully resisted all the attempts of the enemy to break through. In calling attention to these figures, it is not intended in any sense to draw invidious comparisons between the relative merits of the French and British soldier, or even to suggest that the British troops accomplished a task of which the French would have been incapable. It is generally admitted by all our commanders at the front that the Frenchman as a fighter is unsurpassed, though his methods of fighting are not the same as ours; and, allowing for the fact that, in cases where the entire manhood of a nation fights, the average of individual excellence must obviously be lower than when only a select body of volunteers is engaged, for explanatory purposes with regard to the disposition of troops, one may safely reckon a French and British regiment as being of equal fighting value.

All that is aimed at, then, is to try and bring to the mind of the reader, by a comparison of figures, some grasp of the immensity of the performance of our troops east and south of Ypres, during the desperate efforts of the enemy to break through in the last fortnight of October and the first fortnight of November. It is worthy of note, too, that in spite of the huge reinforcements brought up, no material advance was made on the position taken over from us on November 1st. It is true that on the day following, the newly-arrived French troops re-took Wytschate and Messines, from which we had been driven, but they were unable to hold those places, and the line along which they had found us facing the enemy was never perceptibly advanced. The new line at the beginning of November, held jointly by the French troops and British cavalry, ran—roughly speaking—from Klein Zillebeke to Ploegsteert, with a concave face which skirted Hollebeke, Wytschate, and Messines. Our 1st Cavalry Division, supported by some units from the 2nd A.C., was withdrawn to Wulverghem, and the 2nd Cavalry Division went into reserve at Bailleul. Neuve Eglise became our advanced base for that part of the line, and was very quickly packed with British troops.

We have now taken a permanent farewell, as far as these pages are concerned, of all occurrences south of the canal at Hollebeke. We have seen the 2nd A.C. relieved by the Indians, and the cavalry corps relieved by the French, and, with this change of guardianship, we have seen two of the most important points in the line of defence pass out of the keeping of the original Expeditionary Force.

Of that force the 1st A.C. alone (with the 7th Division, which it had absorbed) still remained unrelieved east and south-east of Ypres. The force, however, which now stood between the enemy and the possession of Ypres, had by this time lost many of its distinctive characteristics. The actual battalion units had become in most cases reduced to a mere shadow of their original strength. The 7th Division had become part of the 1st A.C., and several battalions of the 2nd A.C. were acting in concert with this already mixed corps. Many of the brigades had been broken up from their original constituents, and the fragments consolidated into new and temporary brigades. Sir Horace was for the moment an A.C. commander without an A.C., the remnants of his six heroic brigades being scattered here and there along the whole front.

The first, and perhaps the most interesting, because the most strenuous, epoch in the war—as far as it concerned the British force—was nearly closed; but not quite. Before that can be written of it, some great deeds had yet to be done, and were done. The Germans were still making continuous and determined efforts to break through to Ypres by way of Klein Zillebeke, and to that particular zone of the fighting our attention can henceforth be confined.

CHAPTER 29

Klein Zillebeke

When we last took leave of the Klein Zillebeke section of the fighting line, on the night of October 30th, the cavalry position from Klein Zillebeke to the canal had just been taken over by Lord Cavan with the 2nd Grenadiers and Irish Guards, the former being on the canal. On the left of the Irish Guards were the 2nd Gordon Highlanders, with the Oxford Light Infantry in reserve, and beyond them the Sussex and Northamptons, with their left joining up with the 22nd Brigade. On the left of the 22nd Brigade was the 21st Brigade, with the 2nd R. Scots Fusiliers on its extreme flank just south of the Menin road at Gheluvelt. The 20th Brigade was in reserve.

During the morning the 3rd Cavalry Division was kept at Verbranden Molen ready for emergencies, but about 1 p.m. orders were received for it to go to the support of the 3rd C.B. at St. Eloi. Contradictory orders were, however, afterwards received, and in the end the brigade joined up with the 4th Hussars, and together they held the two bridges over the canal at the bend just north of Hollebeke till nightfall. In this action Sergeant Seddons, of the 4th Hussars, showed great gallantry during the defence of the eastern bridge and was deservedly awarded the D.C.M. In the meanwhile the 6th C.B. was sent along the Menin road so as to be ready to co-operate with the 7th Division or the 1st A.C. in case of need. That need—as will presently be seen—very quickly arose.

The original plan for this day had been to attack and retake the Zandvoorde ridge, together with the trenches which had been lost the day before, but the enemy's extreme activity rendered this impracticable, and we were in the end forced to act purely on the defensive.

We are now, be it remembered, dealing with the morning of October 31st, the day on which the cavalry were driven out of Wytschate and Messines and the 1st and 7th Divisions out of Gheluvelt. The terrific bombardment of that morning has already been described. It was chiefly concentrated on the Menin road, but the whole line from Gheluvelt to the canal was involved.

The 2nd Brigade, which was between the two Guards' battalions and the 7th Division, had a curious experience during the morning. It survived the bombardment, and when this slackened to allow the German infantry to advance, it was still in its trenches and prepared to remain there. About eight o'clock, however, General Bulfin summoned the four C.Os of the brigade, and ordered a general retirement of the brigade to the cross-roads at Zillebeke, about a mile in rear. This was duly carried out, and without much loss on the part of the Sussex and Northamptons, who were able to retire through the Zwartelen woods without coming under observation. The 2nd Gordon Highlanders, however (attached temporarily to the 2nd Brigade), were less fortunate. Their trenches were in the open, running north-eastward from Klein Zillebeke farm along the edge of the country lane known as the Brown Road, and, in retiring, they had to cross a considerable tract of exposed ground, during which they suffered very severely from machine-gun fire, Captain McLean's company being practically wiped out.

It was afterwards freely rumoured that this order to retire had been delivered to General Bulfin, as a Divisional Order, by a German dressed in the uniform of a British Staff officer. Some colour is given to this rumour by the extreme improbability of such an order having been officially given after Sir Douglas Haig's ultimatum of the day before, that the line which this apocryphal order caused to be abandoned was to be held at all costs. In any event, it is a matter of history that those concerned did not accept the retired position as a permanency, and a counter-attack was quickly organized. The 6th C.B., which had been waiting in reserve on the Menin road, was brought up as far as the Basseville brook, where they deployed to the south, and, partly mounted and partly dismounted, charged through the Zwartelen woods. Simultaneously the Gordon Highlanders, now reduced to 300, and under the command of Major Craufurd (Colonel Uniacke having been knocked out by a shell

176

earlier in the day), charged on the right of the cavalry, with the Oxford Light Infantry extending the line again on their right. Before this united movement the Bavarian troops in the woods turned and ran, but, true to their principles, continued to cover their retreat with a heavy machine-gun fire. Two of these machine-guns were successfully located, and the 6th C.B. manhandled a gun into the firing line and knocked them both out in fine style. This broke the back of the resistance. The Bavarians started surrendering, and the Gordon Highlanders took a number of prisoners up to the time when Lieutenant Grahame was shot dead by an officer who had surrendered to him; after that they took fewer.

The enemy losses were very heavy. Eight hundred and seventy prisoners were taken during the day, and the number of killed and wounded in the woods ran into several hundreds.

This charge—successful though it had been in clearing the Zwartelen woods of the enemy—had not yet reinstated the 2nd Brigade in the line which they had occupied in the morning, before the much-discussed order to retire had arisen. General Bulfin therefore decided to try during the night to regain the morning position. Accordingly at midnight, under the full moon, and at the same time that the desperate battle was raging round Messines and Wytschate eight miles to the south-west, the 2nd Brigade made their second counter-attack. This, as far as it went, was a complete success. The trenches were carried and occupied, and the Germans driven out. Unfortunately, however, the 22nd Brigade, on the left, found themselves unable to get up into line, and, owing to their left being unprotected, the 2nd Brigade battalions had one after the other—in succession from the left—to fall back again.

These two attacks, *i.e.*, the afternoon charge through the woods and the midnight assault on the trenches, had now reduced the Gordons to 3 officers and 110 men, and these were for the time being amalgamated with the Oxfordshire Light Infantry, who were on their right. The Irish Guards remained in their original position, on the right of the Oxfordshire Light Infantry, but the 2nd Grenadiers were relieved by French Territorials and went back into reserve.

The net result of this terrible day's fighting was that our line was pushed back everywhere, except at Klein Zillebeke and Zonnebeke, the two points which marked the northern and southern limits of the Ypres salient. The effect of the recapture of the Gheluvelt position by the 2nd Worcesters and 1st Scots Guards was neutralized by the cave in the line south of that place, which rendered Gheluvelt untenable. It had therefore to be abandoned. The loss of that place, however, was of no material importance, as its abandonment had long been recognized as a necessary step in the gradual straightening out of the Ypres salient. The only serious effect of the new line was that Klein Zillebeke, which for long had been the re-entering angle, so to speak, of the position, now, by the retirements to right and left of it, was pushed forward into a species of salient, and its vulnerability was thereby appreciably increased. This increased vulnerability at once transformed Klein Zillebeke into the centre of interest as far as this zone was concerned, this little village being—for reasons already given—a spot which at any and all costs had to be kept from the enemy. To Klein Zillebeke and neighbourhood, then, we may not unreasonably look for early developments.

One of the many unhappy incidents of this day's costly fighting was the landing of a shell in the Divisional headquarters at Hooge, by which General Lomax received wounds from which he subsequently died, General Munro was rendered unconscious, and Colonel Kerr and five staff officers were killed.

CHAPTER 30

The Relief of the Seventh Division

All through the 31st and morning following, the Irish Guards on the right of the Gordon Highlanders were subjected to a relentless shelling, and their casualties were considerable. On the morning of November 1st both their machine-guns were knocked out, and at 3 p.m. news came that they were retiring. Lord Cavan sent word for them to hold on some 200 yards to the rear, and also for the French Territorials between them and the canal at Hollebeke to hold on to their position at all costs. This the French managed to do, with very great credit to themselves, at the same time throwing back their left so as to keep in touch with the new position.

The Germans at once occupied the Irish Guards' trenches, but luckily did not realize the position sufficiently to pursue their advantage further, otherwise the consequences might have been serious. As it was, sufficient time was given for the 2nd Grenadiers and 7th C.B. to come up in support, and with this stiffening the new line was held for the rest of the day. But there was a cave at Klein Zillebeke.

The Irish Guards had 400 casualties during this and the previous day's fighting, including 11 officers: Major Stepney, the Hon. A. Mulholland and Lieutenants Coke and Mathieson being killed, and Colonel Lord Ardee (attached from the Grenadiers), the Hon. T. Vesey, the Hon. A. Alexander, Lieutenants Fergusson, Gore-Langton, Lord Kingston, and Lord Francis Scott (attached from Grenadiers), wounded. The last named officer and Captain Orr-Ewing (attached from Scots Guards) were each awarded the D.S.O. "for gallant and persistent attempts to rally the battalion."

On the morning of November 2nd there was a renewal of the regulation attack along the Menin road. This time the attack took the form of a high-explosive bombardment of the barricade across the road at Veldhoek. This was soon demolished and an infantry attack on the 1st Brigade ensued, as a result of which that skeleton brigade yielded 300 yards of ground, but held on to the trenches in rear till nightfall.

Further south, about 11.30 on the same morning, a tremendous attack was delivered against the 2nd Brigade, in the course of which General Bulfin was wounded and part of the line driven in. An urgent appeal for support was sent to Lord Cavan, upon whom it now devolved to take over command of General Bulfin's four battalions, in addition to his own two. He made his way with all speed to the scene of action, with a view to discovering the extent of the mischief. This proved to be (so far) that the Northamptons had been driven in, and that the enemy—following up—had broken through in numbers into the Hooge woods. Beyond the Northamptons, that is to say, on the left of his new command, the R. Sussex were still standing firm. This regiment, however, was greatly reduced in numbers, its casualties during the last four days having averaged over a hundred per day. On the 30th Colonel Crispin had been killed; on the following day his successor, Major Green, had been killed, and the regiment was at the moment under the command of Captain Villiers. Lord Cavan found it in an extremely precarious situation, owing to its weak numerical condition, and the envelopment of its right flank, consequent upon the Northamptons' retirement. He thereupon hurried up the 2nd Grenadiers from reserve as far as the Brown Road, where he ordered them to leave their packs and go straight through the wood towards the south-east with the bayonet.

These Ypres woods have all the appearance of an English copse wood, that is to say, they are formed of some six years' growth of hazel and ash, with standard oaks dotted about here and there. Incidentally they were at this time full of pheasants, destined to be shot in normal times by the lords of the *châteaux* of Hooge, Gheluvelt and Heronhage. Precisely in the manner of a line of beaters driving game, the Grenadiers now pushed through the thick undergrowth, and while the pheasants rose before the advancing line, so did the Germans run. By 4.30 the wood was cleared and the morning line restored. The Northamptons thereupon re-occupied their trenches, but they were not destined to be left there in peace. About six in the evening the Germans again attacked the same part of the line, this time advancing with discordant yells, thinking, no doubt, to repeat their performance of the morning. If so, the event must have come to them as something of a surprise, for the Northamptons—profiting possibly by their previous experience—coolly waited till the attacking party was within fifty yards of the trenches, and then mowed them down. Not a German reached the trenches, and over 200 dead were left on the ground.

At night the R. Sussex were brought back into reserve and the remnant of the Gordons went back to the 20th Brigade, which brigade was at the time in the grounds of the Hooge Château. In addition to their previous losses, the Gordons had during the day lost their C.O., Major Craufurd, who was wounded in the early morning. The position of Lord Cavan's command was then, as follows: the Northamptons on the left, in touch with the R. Welsh Fusiliers in the 7th Division; then the Oxfordshire Light Infantry and the 2nd Grenadiers, who had become very much mixed up, and on the right the Irish Guards. Beyond were the French Territorials.

With the fall of night on the 2nd of November the acuteness of the five days' crisis may be said to have passed. The all-highest warlord had come and gone; the supreme effort of the enemy to break through to Ypres had been made, and had failed; the British force had come out of the ordeal reduced to a shadow, and battered out of recognition, but unconquered. The Kaiser's forces had fallen back sullen and—for the time being—disheartened, realizing at last the hopelessness of the task they had been set to accomplish. Their losses had been prodigious, and though their repeated attacks had—at great sacrifice—forced back the face of the Ypres salient some two miles, the only military effect resulting therefrom was that the British force was at last in occupation of the true line of defence dictated by military prudence and the natural features of the country. From this line, that is to say, the ridge some 150 feet in height which runs from the corner of the canal at Hollebeke to Zonnebeke, they were never afterwards dislodged.

The 3rd, 4th and 5th were in the main uneventful. November 5th was chiefly memorable in this year, not for anti-Popish demonstrations, but as the day on which the 7th Division—after three weeks' incessant fighting—was temporarily relieved. During the three weeks in question it had lost 356 officers out of a full complement of 400, and 9,664 rank and file out of a total of 12,000. Battalions had been reduced to the dimensions of platoons, and had, in some cases, lost every combatant officer.

The 7th Division's performance, during its three weeks east of Ypres, will go down to history as one of the most remarkable achievements in the records of war. Many other units had, by the second half of November, lost as heavily in officers and men as had the twelve battalions of the 7th Division—in one or two cases even more heavily; but the losses of these had been distributed over three months; those of the 7th Division were concentrated into three weeks. They had been suddenly pitchforked into a position of the most supreme responsibility. They found themselves more by chance than by design standing in the road along which the warlord had elected to make his most determined efforts to reach Calais. These efforts came as a succession of hammer-blows, which gave the defending force neither rest nor respite, and to cope with which their numbers were ludicrously insufficient. Their failure, however, would have spelt disaster to the cause of the Allies, and—realizing this—they actually achieved the impossible. There is something particularly stirring in the thought of this small force beaten back step by step, as fresh and fresh troops were hurled upon it day after day, and yet never turning its back to the foe, never beaten, never despondent, and never for a moment failing in the trust which had been imposed upon it. The most remarkable feature about the 7th Division was that it had no weak spot in its composition. Each one of its twelve battalions lived up in every particular to the high standard of duty and efficiency which the Division set itself from the beginning. The troops were mostly veterans from abroad, who had been summoned back from foreign service too late to take part in the earlier stages of the war, and they may therefore in a sense be considered as picked troops.[1]

The 7th and 15th Brigades from the 2nd A.C., who relieved the 7th Division, were themselves sadly thinned in numbers. The 7th Brigade, which took the place of the 20th Brigade, had, in fact, lost seventy-four per cent. of its numbers during the fighting round La Bassée, and was in almost as bad a plight as the 20th Brigade, which it relieved. The 15th Brigade, which replaced the 22nd, was rather stronger, having received drafts from home.

The 20th Brigade went back to Locre, and the 22nd to Bailleul. The 21st—which perhaps had suffered rather the least of the three—remained for the time being in the trenches.

At night the 6th C.B. took over the trenches at Heronhage Château from the 3rd Brigade, who had been having a rough time during the preceding days, and these went back into reserve.

---

1. The 7th Division (General Capper). 20th Brigade (General Ruggles-Brise), 1st Grenadiers. 2nd Scots Guards, 2nd Battalion the Border Regiment. 2nd Gordon Highlanders (old 92nd).
21st Brigade (General Watt), 2nd Yorkshire Regiment. 2nd Bedfordshire Regiment, 2nd R. Scots Fusiliers. 2nd Wiltshire Regiment.
22nd Brigade (General Lawford), 2nd R. Warwickshire Regiment. 2nd Queen's (R. West Surrey Regiment), 1st R. Welsh Fusiliers. 1st S. Staffordshire Regiment.

CHAPTER 31

Zwartelen

November 6th saw a certain renewal of the enemy's activity. The day opened very foggy, but by eleven o'clock there was a bright sun. In the morning the French once more re-took Wytschate and Messines, but again found them untenable, and in fact this was the last attempt on the part of the Allies to occupy either of these two places.

The respite of the poor 22nd Brigade from the trenches was short-lived, and the evening of the 6th saw them once more hurried up into the firing line. This came about in the following way. The French had now taken over all our trenches as far north as the Brown Road, our own troops being pushed up to the left. North of the French were the Irish Guards, and, beyond them, the 2nd Grenadiers. The French troops, who had so far held their ground with splendid tenacity, now found the position more than they could support. The German bombardment, with which they as usual opened the day, was more than usually severe, and lasted the whole morning, and about 2 p.m. it was followed by an infantry attack before which the left of the French and the right of the Irish Guards was driven in. As a result of this cave in the line, the left of the Irish Guards, which remained in the trenches, suffered considerably, Lord John Hamilton, Captain King-Harman and Lieutenant Woodroffe being killed. An urgent message was sent to General Kavanagh to bring up the 7th C.B., who were in readiness near Lord Cavan's headquarters behind Zillebeke, and the 22nd Brigade was also wired for to come up from Bailleul. The cavalry came galloping up to Zillebeke, where they dismounted and advanced on foot along and astride of the road from Zillebeke to Zwartelen, which runs along the foot of the ridge ending in Hill 60. Just short of Zwartelen they deployed, the 1st Life Guards on the left being told off to restore the Irish Guards' position, while the 2nd Life Guards attacked the position from which the French had been driven. The Blues were behind the centre of the line in support.

The 1st Life Guards, under the Hon. A. Stanley, attacked the lost trenches of the Irish Guards with the greatest vigour, and within an hour had regained, at the point of the bayonet, the whole of the position lost. The Hon. A. Stanley received the medal for Distinguished Service for his conduct on this occasion, as did also Corporal Baillie and Corporal Fleming. Sergeant Munn, of the Irish Guards, also got the D.C.M. for rallying some men of his battalion and joining in the charge of the 1st Life Guards.

In the meanwhile the Hon. Hugh Dawnay, commanding the 2nd Life Guards, sent off "B" Squadron to connect up with the right of the 1st Life Guards and clear the wood on the Klein Zillebeke ridge. "D" Squadron was sent off to cover the right flank of the whole combined movement by advancing along the edge of the Ypres to Armentières railway, which is separated from the wood by about 500 yards of open ground; while Major Dawnay himself, with "C" Troop, attacked the village of Zwartelen, with the Blues under Colonel Wilson on his left, and some 300 of the French, who—encouraged by the advance of the Household Cavalry—had reformed, on his right, that is to say, between him and "D" Squadron on the railway.

The whole scheme worked admirably. The attack by "B" Squadron on the Klein Zillebeke ridge wood was entirely successful, the enemy being driven out with loss and pursued for several hundred yards. The attack on Zwartelen—though perhaps a more formidable undertaking—was no less successful. The village was very strongly held, the houses in and around being occupied and defended, and the Household Cavalry's advance was met by a heavy rifle fire which caused many casualties, both Colonel Wilson and Major Dawnay being killed while leading their respective regiments. In spite of heavy losses, however, the cavalrymen, with great steadiness and determination, pressed home their attack, and, at the point of the bayonet, carried the village and captured a number of prisoners, "C" Troop of the 2nd Life Guards afterwards pushing right through and occupying the trenches in the wood on the far side of the village. Lieutenant Stewart-Menzies, Corporal Watt, Corporal Moulsen and Corporal Anstice were all decorated for their gallantry during this brilliant performance on the part of "C" Troop. The latter N.C.O. displayed the greatest courage throughout the fight.

The success of the counter-attack was now to all appearances complete, all the ground lost in the morning having been regained. At this moment, however, the French on the right of "C" Troop again gave way, leaving a gap into which the enemy at once pressed. The position of "C" Troop was now greatly imperilled, and General Kavanagh ordered the Blues, and "B" Squadron of the 2nd Life Guards, to cross the Verbranden Molen road to its support. This was done, the Blues moving to the right and occupying Zwartelen and Hill 60, and in these several positions the combined force continued to fight out time; but some of the ground which had been regained had to be abandoned.

The situation was saved by the arrival about 6 p.m. of the 22nd Brigade, which had been hurried up from Bailleul in motor-buses. This brigade now took over the Household Cavalry position at Zwartelen, while the 2nd K.R.R., from the 2nd Brigade, relieved the squadron of the 2nd Life Guards which was holding the railway on the right flank.

The Household Cavalry earned the very highest praise for their performance on this afternoon. They were handled with great skill by General Kavanagh, and the daring and dash of their advance undoubtedly averted what might have proved a very serious calamity. They lost seventeen officers during their advance, as follows:

In the 1st Life Guards the Hon. R. Wyndham (attached from the Lincolnshire Yeomanry) was killed and the Hon. H. Denison, the Hon. E. Fitzroy and Captain Hardy were wounded. In the 2nd Life Guards the Hon. H. Dawnay, the Hon. A. O'Neill and Lieutenant Peterson were killed and the Hon. M. Lyon, Lieutenant Jobson, Lieutenant Sandys and 2nd Lieutenant Hobson were wounded.

In the Blues, Colonel Wilson and Lieutenant de Gunzberg were killed, and Lord Gerard, Lord Northampton and Captain Brassey were wounded.

The enemy's bombardment of the morning, and the infantry attack of the afternoon which followed, had by no means been confined to the area the loss and recapture of which has just been described. The 2nd Grenadiers, on the left of the Irish Guards, were as heavily attacked as any, but they succeeded in maintaining their ground throughout both morning and afternoon. Sergeant Thomas, who as Corporal Thomas had so distinguished himself at Chavonne, once again showed the material of which he was made. His trench was subjected to a most appalling shelling. Only two of his platoon remained unwounded; he himself had twice been buried and the flank of his trench was exposed, but even in this apparently impossible position he held on, and was still in proud occupation of his trench when the arrival of the 7th C.B. and 22nd Brigade once more drove back the enemy. Sergeant Holmes and Corporal Harrison in the same battalion also greatly distinguished themselves.

At daybreak on the 7th, in the dull, misty atmosphere of a November morning, the 22nd Brigade deployed for an attempt to regain the position of the day before. This brigade, owing to its depleted condition, was now reduced to two composite battalions, the R. Welsh Fusiliers and 2nd Queen's being amalgamated into one battalion under the command of Captain Alleyne of the Queen's, and the Warwicks and S. Staffords into the other, under the command of Captain Vallentin of the S. Staffords. It is worthy of note that the brigade could furnish no officers of higher rank than a captain; also that both the officers above-named fell on the second day of their command, Captain Alleyne being badly wounded and Captain Vallentin killed. The latter was posthumously awarded the Victoria Cross for the great gallantry he had displayed in the command of his composite battalion.

The brigade deployed in four lines, of which the first two were formed by the 2nd Queen's, who now numbered about 400. In this formation they advanced till within 300 yards of the enemy's position, when the first two lines joined up and charged. In spite of a heavy machine-gun fire, which still further reduced the 400, the Queen's charged right home and in rapid succession carried first one and then a second line of trenches, the defenders being all bayoneted or put to flight. The second of these two positions—the same, in fact, as had been captured by the 2nd Life Guards the day before—proved to be too far ahead of the general line and had to be abandoned, as it was persistently enfiladed by machine-gun fire from a farm-house on the left; but the first line was successfully held till night, when the battalion was relieved. During this charge of the Queen's Lieutenant Haigh was killed and Captain Alleyne, Captain Roberts, Lieutenants Lang-Browne, Collis and Pascoe were wounded. Three machine-guns were captured.

The 22nd Brigade was now reduced to four officers, that is to say, one to each battalion, and at night they were finally relieved, and allowed to return to the retirement from which they had been so rudely summoned.

During this same day there was some severe fighting in the Polygon wood, the Connaught Rangers being driven back and their trenches captured. The flank of the Coldstream Brigade thus became threatened, and for a time the position promised to be serious, but the 6th Brigade on the Zonnebeke road came to the rescue, the lost trenches were regained, and the continuity of the line once more established.

The morning of the 8th saw a renewal of the attempt to break through along the Menin road. At the first assault the French and two companies of the Loyal N. Lancashire Regiment in the first line were driven back, and the flank of the 1st Scots Guards became exposed. As a result the enemy was able to rake the trenches of the latter regiment with machine-guns and their casualties were heavy, Lieutenants Cripps, Stirling-Stuart, Monckton and Smith being killed. The battalion, however, held on till the morning position was once more restored by the two reserve companies of the Loyal N. Lancashires, who, counter-attacking with great spirit and determination, drove back the enemy from the position they had temporarily won.

CHAPTER 32

The Prussian Guard Attack

From November 8th to 11th there was little fighting. It had been apparently realized at length by the German commanders that the troops they were at present employing were incapable of breaking the British line, but at the back of that admission there was evidently still the belief that the task was possible, provided the troops employed were sufficiently good. Accordingly the Prussian Guard was sent for. Pending the arrival of that invincible body there was a lull in the ceaseless hammer of battle; and in the meanwhile the weather changed for the worse. By the time the Prussian Guard was ready for its enterprise, that is to say by November 11th, it was about as bad as it could be. A strong west wind was accompanied by an icy rain, which fell all day in torrents. Luckily the wind and rain were in the faces of the enemy, a factor of no little importance.

The battle of November 11th may be looked upon as the last attempt but one of the Germans to break through to Calais during the 1914 campaign. The actual last serious attempt was on November 17th. On the 11th the cannonade began at daybreak and was kept up till 9.30. In violence and volume it rivalled that of October 31st. The entire front from Klein Zillebeke to Zonnebeke was involved, the enemy's design being—as on the 31st—to attack all along the front simultaneously so as to hamper and cripple the British commanders in the use of the very limited reserves at their disposal.

The newly-arrived troops were the 1st and 4th Brigade Prussian Guard, and some battalions of the Garde Jäger, in all fifteen battalions, and to these was entrusted the main attack on the key of the position, *i.e.*, along, and north of, the Menin road.

The Prussian Guard attacked through Veldhoek, and in their advance displayed the invincible courage for which they have ever been famed. Such courage, however—though sufficiently sublime from the spectacular point of view—cannot fail to be expensive, and the losses among these gallant men were prodigious. It was afterwards said by a prisoner that they had been deceived by the silence in our trenches into thinking that the bombardment had cleared them, and so came on recklessly. However, in spite of their losses, by sheer intrepidity and weight of numbers, they succeeded in capturing all the front line trenches of the 1st Brigade, who were astride the Menin road between Veldhoek and Hooge. In three places large bodies of the enemy succeeded in breaking through, and in each case their success furnished a subject for reflection as to the why and the wherefore of battles. For, having succeeded in doing that which they had set out to do, they stood huddled together in the plainest uncertainty as to how next to act, a point which was speedily settled by the arrival of our reserves, who fell upon the successful invaders and promptly annihilated them. One party of some 700 were accounted for to a man by the Oxfordshire Light Infantry, led by Colonel Davies.

Another party which had broken through in the Polygon wood was similarly dealt with by the Highland Light Infantry under Colonel Wolfe-Murray, an operation during which Lieutenant Brodie won the Victoria Cross for exceptional gallantry. This was the second Victoria Cross to fall to this battalion,[1] which had indeed never failed in any situation which it had been called upon to face. General Willcocks, in subsequently addressing the battalion, alluded with pride to "the magnificent glory" with which it had fought, and concluded with the remarkable words: "There is no position which the Highland Light Infantry cannot capture."

The net result of the day's fighting was that the enemy gained some 500 yards of ground, which, from the military point of view, advantaged them nothing, and the gaining of which had cost them some thousands of their best men. The barrenness of the advance made cannot be better illustrated than by the fact that it was the last step forward of the invading army, till the asphyxiating gas was brought into play in the spring of 1915.

1. Private Wilson had gained the honour on September 14th.

On the 12th the 1st Brigade, which had borne the brunt of the Prussian Guard attack, was taken back into reserve. It will be conceded that it was about time.

This gallant Brigade, 4,500 strong in August, was now represented as follows:

1st Scots Guards: Captain Stracey and 69 men. Black Watch: Captain Fortune and 109 men. Camerons: Colonel McEwen, Major Craig-Browne, Lieutenant Dunsterville and 140 men. 1st Coldstream: No officers and 150 men.

The 6th C.B. was now reinforced by the arrival of the North Somerset and Leicestershire Yeomanry Regiments. This strengthening was sorely needed, the brigade having been practically without rest since its arrival in Flanders. By the irony of fate the Hon. W. Cadogan, the Colonel of the 10th Hussars, was killed on the very day when these reinforcements arrived.

With this addition to its strength the brigade was now required to find 800 rifles for its line of trenches along the Klein Zillebeke ridge, and in addition to furnish a reserve of 400, who—when not required—lived in burrows in the railway cutting at Hooge. Within a week, however, the reserve became a luxury of the past, and the brigade was called upon to find 1,200 rifles for the trenches.

On November 17th we come to the last serious attempt of the enemy, during the 1914 campaign, to break through to Calais by way of Ypres. This final effort can be dismissed in a few words. It was made south of the Menin road by the XV. German Army Corps, and it took the form of two infantry attacks, one at 1 p.m. and another at 4 p.m.; and it failed utterly, the Germans leaving thousands of dead and wounded on the ground just in front of our trenches, to which they had been allowed to approach quite close.

The signal failure of this last spasmodic effort, and the subsequent passivity of the enemy, points with some significance to the conclusion that the position to which we had now been driven back along the Zillebeke—Zonnebeke ridge was impregnable, and was recognized as such by the enemy.

The 6th C.B. and the 2nd Grenadiers were the most prominent figures in this victory of November 17th. In the course of the second attack the 10th Hussars and 3rd Dragoon Guards allowed the enemy to come within a few yards of their trenches before they opened fire and mowed them down in masses. The 10th Hussars, however, again suffered somewhat severely in officers, the Hon. A. Annesley, Captain Peto, and Lieutenant Drake being killed. The newly-arrived North Somerset Yeomanry, under Colonel Glyn, behaved with the coolness and steadiness of veterans, and contributed in no small degree to the repulse of the enemy's second attack.

The 2nd Grenadiers received the highest praise from Lord Cavan for their part in this day's fighting. This battalion had now lost 30 officers and 1,300 men since the beginning of the campaign, and on the following day it was sent back into reserve to recoup and reorganize.

Epitaph

With the German failure of November 17th the first chapter in the Great War may be considered closed. The desperate and all but uninterrupted fighting which, for three months, followed the defence of the Mons canal, was succeeded by a long lull, during which both sides were busily engaged fighting a common foe. The winter of 1914 proved the wettest in the memory of man, and ague, rheumatism, frost-bite, gangrene and tetanus filled the hospitals with little less regularity than had the shot and shell of the autumn. Then came the great battle of Neuve Chapelle, and in another part of the world the grim struggles of the Dardanelles. These are another story, and some day this will be told; but great as may have been—and undoubtedly has been—the glory won in other fields, nothing can ever surpass, as a story of simple, sublime pluck, the history of the first three months of England's participation in the Great War.

The word "pluck" is used with intention, for it conveys, perhaps, better than any other word a sense of that indomitable spirit which is superior to every rub of adverse fortune. There were no war correspondents present with the First Expeditionary Force. There was no wrapping of specially favoured deeds in tinsel for the eyes of a cheap gallery. Even if the wrappers had been present, the general standard was too high for invidious selection. A mole-hill stands out on a plain, but makes no show in the uplands. V.Cs, it is true, were won; but for every one given a hundred were earned. Military honours are the fruit of recommendation; but when generals, colonels, company officers and sergeants are no more, the deed must be its own record; there is none left to recommend.

The grandeur of the doings of those First Seven Divisions lies, it may well be, in their immunity from the play of a cheap flashlight—a flashlight which too often distorts the perspective, and so illuminates the wrong spot. There is a gospel in the very reticence of the records of the regiments concerned—in the dignity with which, without any blare of trumpets, they tell of the daily answer to the call of a duty which balanced them ceaselessly on the edge of eternity. But it is always told as of a simple response to the call of duty, and not as a thing to be waved in the faces of an audience.

But, though unflattered and unsung, those early deeds in France and Flanders can boast an epitaph which tells no lies, and which, in its simple tragedy, is more eloquent than a volume of strained panegyrics.

The register of "missing" is an enigma; it may mean many things. But the register of killed and wounded is no enigma. It tells, in the simplest terms, a tale of death and mutilation faced and found at the call of duty. Let us leave it at that.

The First Expeditionary Force is no more. The distinctive names and numbers of the units that composed it still face one from the pages of the "Army List;" but of the bronzed, cheery men who sailed in August, 1914, one third lie under the soil of France and Flanders. Of those that remain, some have been relegated for ever—and of a cruel necessity—to more peaceful pursuits; others—more hopefully convalescent—are looking forward with eagerness to the day when they will once more be fit to answer the call of duty and of country.

LEONAUR

ALSO FROM LEONAUR
AVAILABLE IN SOFTCOVER OR HARDCOVER WITH DUST JACKET

AFGHANISTAN: THE BELEAGUERED BRIGADE *by G. R. Gleig*—An Account of Sale's Brigade During the First Afghan War.

IN THE RANKS OF THE C. I. V *by Erskine Childers*—With the City Imperial Volunteer Battery (Honourable Artillery Company) in the Second Boer War.

THE BENGAL NATIVE ARMY *by F. G. Cardew*—An Invaluable Reference Resource.

THE 7TH (QUEEN'S OWN) HUSSARS: Volume 4—1688-1914 *by C. R. B. Barrett*—Uniforms, Equipment, Weapons, Traditions, the Services of Notable Officers and Men & the Appendices to All Volumes—Volume 4: 1688-1914.

THE SWORD OF THE CROWN *by Eric W. Sheppard*—A History of the British Army to 1914.

THE 7TH (QUEEN'S OWN) HUSSARS: Volume 3—**1818-1914** *by C. R. B. Barrett*—On Campaign During the Canadian Rebellion, the Indian Mutiny, the Sudan, Matabeleland, Mashonaland and the Boer War Volume 3: 1818-1914.

THE KHARTOUM CAMPAIGN *by Bennet Burleigh*—A Special Correspondent's View of the Reconquest of the Sudan by British and Egyptian Forces under Kitchener—1898.

EL PUCHERO *by Richard McSherry*—The Letters of a Surgeon of Volunteers During Scott's Campaign of the American-Mexican War 1847-1848.

RIFLEMAN SAHIB *by E. Maude*—The Recollections of an Officer of the Bombay Rifles During the Southern Mahratta Campaign, Second Sikh War, Persian Campaign and Indian Mutiny.

THE KING'S HUSSAR *by Edwin Mole*—The Recollections of a 14th (King's) Hussar During the Victorian Era.

JOHN COMPANY'S CAVALRYMAN *by William Johnson*—The Experiences of a British Soldier in the Crimea, the Persian Campaign and the Indian Mutiny.

COLENSO & DURNFORD'S ZULU WAR *by Frances E. Colenso & Edward Durnford*—The first and possibly the most important history of the Zulu War.

U. S. DRAGOON *by Samuel E. Chamberlain*—Experiences in the Mexican War 1846-48 and on the South Western Frontier.

LEONAUR

ALSO FROM LEONAUR
AVAILABLE IN SOFTCOVER OR HARDCOVER WITH DUST JACKET

THE FALL OF THE MOGHUL EMPIRE OF HINDUSTAN by H. G. Keene—By the beginning of the nineteenth century, as British and Indian armies under Lake and Wellesley dominated the scene, a little over half a century of conflict brought the Moghul Empire to its knees.

LADY SALE'S AFGHANISTAN by Florentia Sale—An Indomitable Victorian Lady's Account of the Retreat from Kabul During the First Afghan War.

THE CAMPAIGN OF MAGENTA AND SOLFERINO 1859 by Harold Carmichael Wylly—The Decisive Conflict for the Unification of Italy.

FRENCH'S CAVALRY CAMPAIGN by J. G. Maydon—A Special Correspondent's View of British Army Mounted Troops During the Boer War.

CAVALRY AT WATERLOO by Sir Evelyn Wood—British Mounted Troops During the Campaign of 1815.

THE SUBALTERN by George Robert Gleig—The Experiences of an Officer of the 85th Light Infantry During the Peninsular War.

NAPOLEON AT BAY, 1814 by F. Loraine Petre—The Campaigns to the Fall of the First Empire.

NAPOLEON AND THE CAMPAIGN OF 1806 by Colonel Vachée—The Napoleonic Method of Organisation and Command to the Battles of Jena & Auerstädt.

THE COMPLETE ADVENTURES IN THE CONNAUGHT RANGERS by William Grattan—The 88th Regiment during the Napoleonic Wars by a Serving Officer.

BUGLER AND OFFICER OF THE RIFLES by William Green & Harry Smith—With the 95th (Rifles) during the Peninsular & Waterloo Campaigns of the Napoleonic Wars.

NAPOLEONIC WAR STORIES by Sir Arthur Quiller-Couch—Tales of soldiers, spies, battles & sieges from the Peninsular & Waterloo campaingns.

CAPTAIN OF THE 95TH (RIFLES) by Jonathan Leach—An officer of Wellington's sharpshooters during the Peninsular, South of France and Waterloo campaigns of the Napoleonic wars.

RIFLEMAN COSTELLO by Edward Costello—The adventures of a soldier of the 95th (Rifles) in the Peninsular & Waterloo Campaigns of the Napoleonic wars.

LEONAUR

ALSO FROM LEONAUR

AVAILABLE IN SOFTCOVER OR HARDCOVER WITH DUST JACKET

OFFICERS & GENTLEMEN *by Peter Hawker & William Graham*—Two Accounts of British Officers During the Peninsula War: Officer of Light Dragoons by Peter Hawker & Campaign in Portugal and Spain by William Graham .

THE WALCHEREN EXPEDITION *by Anonymous*—The Experiences of a British Officer of the 81st Regt. During the Campaign in the Low Countries of 1809.

LADIES OF WATERLOO *by Charlotte A. Eaton, Magdalene de Lancey & Juana Smith*—The Experiences of Three Women During the Campaign of 1815: Waterloo Days by Charlotte A. Eaton, A Week at Waterloo by Magdalene de Lancey & Juana's Story by Juana Smith.

JOURNAL OF AN OFFICER IN THE KING'S GERMAN LEGION *by John Frederick Hering*—Recollections of Campaigning During the Napoleonic Wars.

JOURNAL OF AN ARMY SURGEON IN THE PENINSULAR WAR *by Charles Boutflower*—The Recollections of a British Army Medical Man on Campaign During the Napoleonic Wars.

ON CAMPAIGN WITH MOORE AND WELLINGTON *by Anthony Hamilton*—The Experiences of a Soldier of the 43rd Regiment During the Peninsular War.

THE ROAD TO AUSTERLITZ *by R. G. Burton*—Napoleon's Campaign of 1805.

SOLDIERS OF NAPOLEON *by A. J. Doisy De Villargennes & Arthur Chuquet*—The Experiences of the Men of the French First Empire: Under the Eagles by A. J. Doisy De Villargennes & Voices of 1812 by Arthur Chuquet .

INVASION OF FRANCE, 1814 *by F. W. O. Maycock*—The Final Battles of the Napoleonic First Empire.

LEIPZIG—A CONFLICT OF TITANS *by Frederic Shoberl*—A Personal Experience of the 'Battle of the Nations' During the Napoleonic Wars, October 14th-19th, 1813.

SLASHERS *by Charles Cadell*—The Campaigns of the 28th Regiment of Foot During the Napoleonic Wars by a Serving Officer.

BATTLE IMPERIAL *by Charles William Vane*—The Campaigns in Germany & France for the Defeat of Napoleon 1813-1814.

SWIFT & BOLD *by Gibbes Rigaud*—The 60th Rifles During the Peninsula War.

LEONAUR
ALSO FROM LEONAUR
AVAILABLE IN SOFTCOVER OR HARDCOVER WITH DUST JACKET

OMPTEDA OF THE KING'S GERMAN LEGION by *Christian von Ompteda*—A Hanoverian Officer on Campaign Against Napoleon.

LIEUTENANT SIMMONS OF THE 95TH (RIFLES) by *George Simmons*—Recollections of the Peninsula, South of France & Waterloo Campaigns of the Napoleonic Wars.

A HORSEMAN FOR THE EMPEROR by *Jean Baptiste Gazzola*—A Cavalryman of Napoleon's Army on Campaign Throughout the Napoleonic Wars.

SERGEANT LAWRENCE by *William Lawrence*—With the 40th Regt. of Foot in South America, the Peninsular War & at Waterloo.

CAMPAIGNS WITH THE FIELD TRAIN by *Richard D. Henegan*—Experiences of a British Officer During the Peninsula and Waterloo Campaigns of the Napoleonic Wars.

CAVALRY SURGEON by *S. D. Broughton*—On Campaign Against Napoleon in the Peninsula & South of France During the Napoleonic Wars 1812-1814.

MEN OF THE RIFLES by *Thomas Knight, Henry Curling & Jonathan Leach*—The Reminiscences of Thomas Knight of the 95th (Rifles) by Thomas Knight, Henry Curling's Anecdotes by Henry Curling & The Field Services of the Rifle Brigade from its Formation to Waterloo by Jonathan Leach.

THE ULM CAMPAIGN 1805 by *F. N. Maude*—Napoleon and the Defeat of the Austrian Army During the 'War of the Third Coalition'.

SOLDIERING WITH THE 'DIVISION' by *Thomas Garrety*—The Military Experiences of an Infantryman of the 43rd Regiment During the Napoleonic Wars.

SERGEANT MORRIS OF THE 73RD FOOT by *Thomas Morris*—The Experiences of a British Infantryman During the Napoleonic Wars-Including Campaigns in Germany and at Waterloo.

A VOICE FROM WATERLOO by *Edward Cotton*—The Personal Experiences of a British Cavalryman Who Became a Battlefield Guide and Authority on the Campaign of 1815.

NAPOLEON AND HIS MARSHALS by *J. T. Headley*—The Men of the First Empire.

LEONAUR

ALSO FROM LEONAUR
AVAILABLE IN SOFTCOVER OR HARDCOVER WITH DUST JACKET

BUGEAUD: A PACK WITH A BATON by *Thomas Robert Bugeaud*—The Early Campaigns of a Soldier of Napoleon's Army Who Would Become a Marshal of France.

WATERLOO RECOLLECTIONS by *Frederick Llewellyn*—Rare First Hand Accounts, Letters, Reports and Retellings from the Campaign of 1815.

SERGEANT NICOL by *Daniel Nicol*—The Experiences of a Gordon Highlander During the Napoleonic Wars in Egypt, the Peninsula and France.

THE JENA CAMPAIGN: 1806 by *F. N. Maude*—The Twin Battles of Jena & Auerstadt Between Napoleon's French and the Prussian Army.

PRIVATE O'NEIL by *Charles O'Neil*—The recollections of an Irish Rogue of H. M. 28th Regt.—The Slashers—during the Peninsula & Waterloo campaigns of the Napoleonic war.

ROYAL HIGHLANDER by *James Anton*—A soldier of H.M 42nd (Royal) Highlanders during the Peninsular, South of France & Waterloo Campaigns of the Napoleonic Wars.

CAPTAIN BLAZE by *Elzéar Blaze*—Life in Napoleons Army.

LEJEUNE VOLUME 1 by *Louis-François Lejeune*—The Napoleonic Wars through the Experiences of an Officer on Berthier's Staff.

LEJEUNE VOLUME 2 by *Louis-François Lejeune*—The Napoleonic Wars through the Experiences of an Officer on Berthier's Staff.

CAPTAIN COIGNET by *Jean-Roch Coignet*—A Soldier of Napoleon's Imperial Guard from the Italian Campaign to Russia and Waterloo.

FUSILIER COOPER by *John S. Cooper*—Experiences in the 7th (Royal) Fusiliers During the Peninsular Campaign of the Napoleonic Wars and the American Campaign to New Orleans.

FIGHTING NAPOLEON'S EMPIRE by *Joseph Anderson*—The Campaigns of a British Infantryman in Italy, Egypt, the Peninsular & the West Indies During the Napoleonic Wars.

CHASSEUR BARRES by *Jean-Baptiste Barres*—The experiences of a French Infantryman of the Imperial Guard at Austerlitz, Jena, Eylau, Friedland, in the Peninsular, Lutzen, Bautzen, Zinnwald and Hanau during the Napoleonic Wars.

LEONAUR

ALSO FROM LEONAUR
AVAILABLE IN SOFTCOVER OR HARDCOVER WITH DUST JACKET

IRON TIMES WITH THE GUARDS *by An O. E. (G. P. A. Fildes)*—The Experiences of an Officer of the Coldstream Guards on the Western Front During the First World War.

THE GREAT WAR IN THE MIDDLE EAST: 1 *by W. T. Massey*—The Desert Campaigns & How Jerusalem Was Won---two classic accounts in one volume.

THE GREAT WAR IN THE MIDDLE EAST: 2 *by W. T. Massey*—Allenby's Final Triumph.

SMITH-DORRIEN *by Horace Smith-Dorrien*—Isandlwhana to the Great War.

1914 *by Sir John French*—The Early Campaigns of the Great War by the British Commander.

GRENADIER *by E. R. M. Fryer*—The Recollections of an Officer of the Grenadier Guards throughout the Great War on the Western Front.

BATTLE, CAPTURE & ESCAPE *by George Pearson*—The Experiences of a Canadian Light Infantryman During the Great War.

DIGGERS AT WAR *by R. Hugh Knyvett & G. P. Cuttriss*—"Over There" With the Australians by R. Hugh Knyvett and Over the Top With the Third Australian Division by G. P. Cuttriss. Accounts of Australians During the Great War in the Middle East, at Gallipoli and on the Western Front.

HEAVY FIGHTING BEFORE US *by George Brenton Laurie*—The Letters of an Officer of the Royal Irish Rifles on the Western Front During the Great War.

THE CAMELIERS *by Oliver Hogue*—A Classic Account of the Australians of the Imperial Camel Corps During the First World War in the Middle East.

RED DUST *by Donald Black*—A Classic Account of Australian Light Horsemen in Palestine During the First World War.

THE LEAN, BROWN MEN *by Angus Buchanan*—Experiences in East Africa During the Great War with the 25th Royal Fusiliers—the Legion of Frontiersmen.

THE NIGERIAN REGIMENT IN EAST AFRICA *by W. D. Downes*—On Campaign During the Great War 1916-1918.

THE 'DIE-HARDS' IN SIBERIA *by John Ward*—With the Middlesex Regiment Against the Bolsheviks 1918-19.

LEONAUR

ALSO FROM LEONAUR
AVAILABLE IN SOFTCOVER OR HARDCOVER WITH DUST JACKET

FARAWAY CAMPAIGN *by F. James*—Experiences of an Indian Army Cavalry Officer in Persia & Russia During the Great War.

REVOLT IN THE DESERT *by T. E. Lawrence*—An account of the experiences of one remarkable British officer's war from his own perspective.

MACHINE-GUN SQUADRON *by A. M. G.*—The 20th Machine Gunners from British Yeomanry Regiments in the Middle East Campaign of the First World War.

A GUNNER'S CRUSADE *by Antony Bluett*—The Campaign in the Desert, Palestine & Syria as Experienced by the Honourable Artillery Company During the Great War .

DESPATCH RIDER *by W. H. L. Watson*—The Experiences of a British Army Motorcycle Despatch Rider During the Opening Battles of the Great War in Europe.

TIGERS ALONG THE TIGRIS *by E. J. Thompson*—The Leicestershire Regiment in Mesopotamia During the First World War.

HEARTS & DRAGONS *by Charles R. M. F. Crutwell*—The 4th Royal Berkshire Regiment in France and Italy During the Great War, 1914-1918.

INFANTRY BRIGADE: 1914 *by John Ward*—The Diary of a Commander of the 15th Infantry Brigade, 5th Division, British Army, During the Retreat from Mons.

DOING OUR 'BIT' *by Ian Hay*—Two Classic Accounts of the Men of Kitchener's 'New Army' During the Great War including *The First 100,000* & *All In It.*

AN EYE IN THE STORM *by Arthur Ruhl*—An American War Correspondent's Experiences of the First World War from the Western Front to Gallipoli-and Beyond.

STAND & FALL *by Joe Cassells*—With the Middlesex Regiment Against the Bolsheviks 1918-19.

RIFLEMAN MACGILL'S WAR *by Patrick MacGill*—A Soldier of the London Irish During the Great War in Europe including *The Amateur Army, The Red Horizon* & *The Great Push.*

WITH THE GUNS *by C. A. Rose & Hugh Dalton*—Two First Hand Accounts of British Gunners at War in Europe During World War 1- Three Years in France with the Guns and With the British Guns in Italy.

THE BUSH WAR DOCTOR *by Robert V. Dolbey*—The Experiences of a British Army Doctor During the East African Campaign of the First World War.